TUTENKHAMEN'S TRACKSUIT

THE HISTORY OF SPORT IN 100ish OBJECTS

D1397739

B L O O M S B U R Y

LONDON · NEW DELHI · NEW YORK · SYDNEY

Tutenkhamen's Tracksuit
The History of Sport in 100ish Objects

First published 2013

Bloomsbury Publishing Plc
50 Bedford Square
London WC1B 3DP
www.bloomsbury.com

Copyright © Alan Tyers and Beach
www.tyersandbeach.com

All rights reserved. No part of this publication may be reproduced in any form or by any means—graphic, electronic, or mechanical, including photocopying, recording, taping or information storage and retrieval systems—without the prior permission in writing of the publishers.

Alan Tyers and Beach have asserted their rights under the Copyright, Design and Patents Acts 1988 to be identified as the authors of this book.

ISBN 978 1 4081 6490 7

A CIP catalogue record for this book is available from the British Library.

This book is produced using paper that is made from wood grown in managed, sustainable forests. It is natural, renewable and recyclable. The logging and manufacturing processes conform to the environmental regulations of the country of origin.

10 9 8 7 6 5 4 3 2 1

Printed and bound in China by C&C Offset Printing Co., Ltd.

GIDEON RUPERT has long been a leading light in the field of sports history. Following the stellar success of his first exhibition, *A Liking for Vikings* (2005), Gideon now finds himself at the helm of the National Museum of the History of Sport in Orkney, where his spirited leadership and a multi-pound refurbishment have helped to push visitor numbers through the three-figure mark for the first time (audit pending). Gideon holds the positions of Senior Curator, Lead Researcher, Principal Archivist and Author-in-chief-in-residence. In his spare time he enjoys sailing, bird-watching and listening to Gaelic rap music.

ALAN TYERS is Acting Junior Researcher at the Museum. Working under Gideon's expert guidance, Alan has been privileged to research the facts behind several of the items in the exhibition (internet connection permitting).

BEACH is the Museum's Assistant Photographic Assistant (Interim). Working carefully with Gideon's new cameraphone, Beach is responsible for some of the simpler images that follow.

Contents

Curator's Statement

ON BEHALF OF ALL at the National Museum of the History of Sport, Orkney, I should like to welcome you to the exhibition catalogue that accompanies our current display, *Tutenkhamen's Tracksuit: The History of Sport in 100ish Objects*. The collection that follows is, I hope, a thorough and exhaustive journey from the beginnings of sporting time right up until the present day. It is also, however, a very personal journey: some of the exhibits come from my own private collection, some of them were lent by colleagues and friends – from Sir Alex Ferguson to the late and much lamented Tupac Shakur. Some of them were procured by means whose specifics I am unable, after legal advice, to discuss fully here.

I had hoped that this foreword might be written by one of two eminent figures, the first from the world of history, the second from the world of sport. I am sorry to say that we were let down rather badly at the last moment by both of them. I can only hope David Starkey will, in years to come, look back on his treachery with shame, although I would not be in the least surprised if he looks back on his treachery and makes one of his awful television programmes about it. Worse yet, we had a cancellation from David Beckham's management company at the eleventh hour saying they were concerned he was becoming over-exposed and that his ghost-writer had been hospitalised with writer's block. It is their loss.

By contrast, however, there have been many others who have been immeasurably supportive and kind in helping to put on this exhibition. It would be impossible to name everyone who has helped with and inspired this collection, so I will limit myself to just two: Tony Adams, for his tireless enthusiasm and piano lessons, and the late Eric Hobsbawm, for helping me set up my laptop.

I very much look welcoming you to the National Museum of the History of Sport, Orkney, and hope that this book pricks your appetite for a visit.

Gideon Rupert, North Ronaldsay, November 2013

Introduction: The Story of Sport

A WINDY, HOT, SEMI-DESERT in north-eastern Africa. 12,000 years ago. A tribe migrates in search of food. As night falls, the group assembles the humble camp, the meagre rations are eaten. Dangers are all around: the climate and terrain, wild animals, unpleasant chafing from the inescapable sand. The women and children huddle for warmth and safety. But the menfolk... the menfolk have other ideas.

Fifty yards from the camp, the remains of a skeleton tell us that among this group was a fellow of about 25. Judging from his bone density and short stature, he was unusually nimble compared to others of his kind. Next to him was found a rock in a crude spherical shape, apparently worked upon to smooth off some of the edges. This is the first evidence we have of an early human ball game, and this an early player.

But further analysis of the skeleton, discovered in 1959 in a joint expedition between the British Museum and Jimmy Hill's Professional Footballers' Association, revealed a sad ending to this charming story of the first soccer players. This primitive footballer's right ankle has been badly broken. Was this man the first victim of a late challenge? Did he, perhaps, skip past a larger, more powerful opponent? If so, it was to be his undoing. The group had no use for a lame male, indeed they simply could not support him. He was left there to die, the sporting object of the rough ball, perhaps sacred in its own right, his one comfort as he passed.

He was buried in a shallow scrape, and the absence of pottery or bones nearby suggests that the group moved on swiftly. It seems a lonely, ignoble death for the first known sportsman, although of course he may have made a meal of the challenge.

So sport was alive, red in tooth and claw: thrilling, dangerous, an escape from the daily grind, sometimes a source of triumph, and for our man with the broken ankle, a road to disaster. But tragedy or joy, it was a distraction in the hostile world of these primitive humans as it is in ours. But why? To answer this question we must go back to the very dawn of creation.

From mankind's earliest days, he had a propensity for play. In pre-agrarian days, simple games allowed man to train his young in the vital disciplines needed to survive: hunting, hiding, shouting at other men. The roots of many of our modern games can be seen in the aiming or striking games played by the first humans.

Indeed, it seems the desire to play with balls for competition and amusement predates even *homo sapiens*. Archaeological findings in Somerset of a primitive shoe that possibly doubled as a drinking cup have caused historians to propose that Neanderthal man may have played a game something like our modern rugby.

Going back further still, there is strong fossil evidence that the dinosaurs may have competed in races to increase their speed. The evolutionary advantages of running fast are self-evident; but more remarkable yet is the possibility that these extraordinary creatures derived something like pleasure or entertainment from their activities. A fossil fragment found in what is now northern Italy suggests that groups of Triceratops may have run in small packs, passing a chewed bone from mouth to mouth like the relay batons of today. The smiling expressions on their massive dinosaur faces suggest that something other than simple exercise was being experienced: sporting satisfaction.

And many physicists believe that the fundamental historical event of them all, the Big Bang, may have been caused by recreation. The eminent Professor David Butcher, Chair of Astrophysics and Match-day Hospitality at Derbyshire County Cricket Club, posits that the way electrons move about with no discernible pattern may be evidence of an indivisible need in all matter for recreational activity. Butcher's Playful Particle may be the greatest discovery yet of astrophysics, supporting as it does the theory that matter whizzing around for its own amusement, competing and racing, may have been the touchstone for life.

The exhibition, *Tutenkhamen's Tracksuit: A History of Sport in 100ish Objects,* traces sport's innovations, its great men and the women behind them, its stories, legends, myths and outrages.

Through an examination of documents, artefacts, buildings and possessions, it illuminates the sporting lives of some of humankind's most famous and important figures – for instance, the prototypical tracksuit worn by Tutenkhamen that is pictured on the cover of this exhibition catalogue. But it also presents sporting chattels of more humble station, for example the roughly-cast Greek amphora that was used to collect urine for the first drug tests, the Dwain chamberpot. From the highest to the lowest, all humankind has played at sport of one kind of another, and the story of humanity is, in effect, the story of sport.

Let us play.

G.R.

The 100ish Objects

1 The Big Bang

Hubble video replay of the act of cosmic creation
The Universe, before kick-off

THE DAWN OF TIME. The dawn of life. The first whistle. The starter's pistol. From this moment everything flowed, stars and planets, life and death, humanity and the offside rule. The Big Bang. The first moment in history.

Or was it? Working at the point where science, religion, sports history and, perhaps, madness all meet, some radical thinkers dare to wonder if the Big Bang may have been caused by *something*. Something so powerful, so fundamental that it predates everything else. And what was that something? It was the need for play.

It is now believed, not by all scientists, but by some, that the Big Bang was brought about by matter trying to escape from a black hole. Does this 'race' to escape represent the first sporting contest? And if so, did 'sport', in fact, create the universe? This still picture from our state-of-the-art Hubble outside broadcast unit at the Museum suggests so.

Of course, some other sporting historians offer what we must call a broadly religious explanation: that the universe was created by someone or something for His own ends. If so, why did this entity do it? He did it, surely, for amusement, to have a pastime, to watch His creation in motion, bursting and competing in all its strange and beguiling glory. And what is that if not sport? And what does this make the Creator, if not the first sports fan?

My own views fall somewhere between the two, a belief in what we might call an Intelligent Sporting Design. Some creator figure saw this matter trying to escape a black hole and thought it had gained an unfair advantage, possibly by tugging at a metaphorical shirt, possibly even by some sort of cosmic doping. Did He explode in rage? Was the Big Bang the first example of crowd unrest? Is the Universe, at root, merely a furious demand for a red card?

As astrophysics, philosophy and video-replay technology currently stand, it is impossible to say with certainty what caused the Big Bang, or who, or why. Of one thing we can be sure: sport had a role to play, and it has been a primary elemental force in life ever since. This book tells that story.

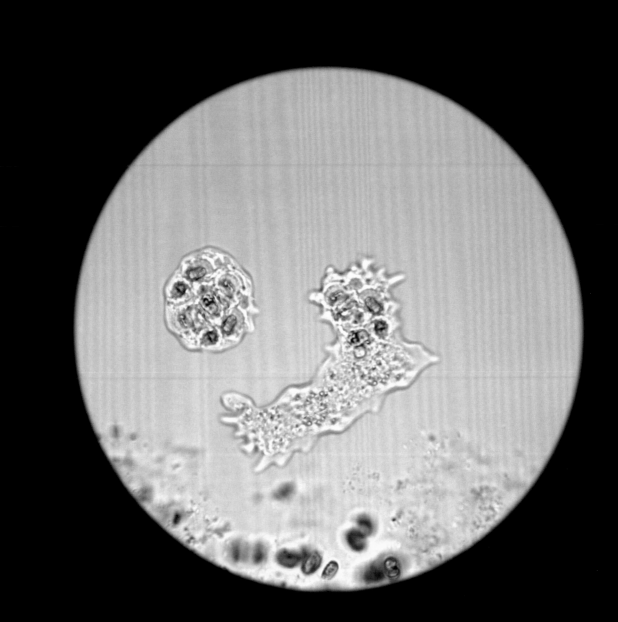

2 The Shola Amoeba

Electron photomicrograph
Sid Waddell Faculty of BioSciences, Tyneside, 600 million years BC

THIS TINY ORGANISM is not just the earliest sporting life on Earth, it is also the oldest. Yet like many of the greatest scientific discoveries, the revelation was stumbled upon quite by accident. In 2002, a University of Tyneside laboratory assistant unknowingly spilled a bottle of Newcastle Brown Ale upon a copy of *Alan Shearer: My Story So Far* during a Christmas party, and left the pulpy alcoholic mixture to ferment over the holiday period.

An elemental state of what scientists now describe as Perfect Geordiness was thus unwittingly recreated under laboratory conditions. Returning after the Christmas break, researchers were astonished and delighted to find a patch of black-and-white striped amoebae, just about visible to the naked eye, growing on the work bench. It seemed that under these highly specific conditions – decaying organic host material at varying degrees of liquidity (very wet pages, very dry book), ethanol and heat; conditions that would come to be known as the Howay Constant – the amoebae were able to expand to a size far greater than previous generations.

Of course, the nature of reproduction by cell division means that these amoebae themselves are in effect the exact same organism, divided again and again, that existed 600 million years ago. Even more remarkably, microscopic investigation reveals them to be not moving around at random, but appearing to do so as if in pursuit of each other. Science has yet to tease out any evolutionary or survival advantage to this whatsoever, therefore we can only conclude that these amoebae are in fact playing, amusing themselves, competing. 600 million years ago, this is what sport looked like. And it looks quite the same today.

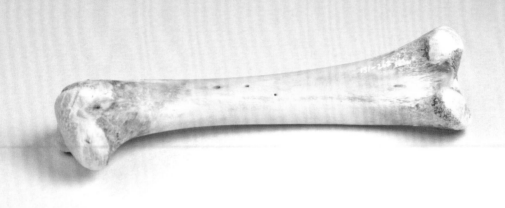

3 Dinosaur Bone

Prehistoric fossil
Sussex, Late Cretaceous period

OF ALL THE OBJECTS in our collection, this is the one with the most personal significance, because it was I myself who discovered it. On a 2004 walking holiday in the South Downs with my cousin Rhoda, we paused to rest on a bench. My eye was drawn to a small white object in the grass; on further inspection it was a bone. Fortune was with me indeed that day, for Rhoda is a keen amateur palaeontologist.

My hands trembling as I picked it up, I knew that we had found something very significant. It was a dinosaur bone, remarkably well preserved, from the knee of a medium-sized carnivore, a contemporary of Tyrannosaurus. The bone is unusual in that it would have given the knee joint a unique flexibility, allowing the dinosaur to leap almost its own height in the air and change direction very suddenly.

According to Rhoda's research and reconstruction from this fossil, the dinosaur would have been 14 feet high, with powerful hind legs and dainty front paws, and it was probably blue. It would have had a notably large number of teeth in a rather small mouth, giving the predator its characteristic 'goofy grin'. It had a mop of hair through which it had to peer, not unlike a West Highland Terrier.

Its springy knees and apparently smiling expression meant that it was largely a happy, playful dinosaur. Some palaeontologists believe that groups may have enjoyed leaping in the air and catching birds in their teeth, which they then threw to each other or hurled into birds' nests for play. In a sense, it was a prehistoric basketballer, although it was not by nature violent towards females.

We have applied to the International Council of Dinosaurs (Online) to have this hugely significant finding named the *Rhodasaurus* but sadly a reply was not received before publication deadline.

Left (top): The bone fragment after extensive cleaning, together with a paleo-forensic artist's impression of what the dinosaur may have looked like (*bottom*).

4 Cave Art

Powdered pigment on rock
Grotte de Meaux-Bottes, Dordogne, c 27000 BC

THIS CAVE, and its superb ancient art of early man running, competing and celebrating victory, was discovered in 2006 by English expatriate Dordogne residents Gerald and Lorraine Waters.

According to an account in the region's local English-language newszine the *Dordogne Britisher* (incorporating the *Périgord Beefeater*), the couple had been 'looking in some deserted caves for a marvellous little local cheesemonger or a charmingly rustic bistro where they serve the wine in earthenware pots and where if you ask for the menu Madame hits you in the face with a goose in the most wonderfully French way', when their Jack Russell terrier, Dacre, slipped his lead and ran underground.

The worried Waterses bravely climbed through a narrow gap in a cave wall to recover the distressed pet, and were rewarded with this magnificent sight: one of the earliest known pieces of rock art, and certainly the first to depict the joy of victory in sporting competition. The figures in the foreground are performing some sort of dance of triumph, probably as a result of having run away from a bison before it killed them.

Mr Waters was kind enough to speak to the Museum about his serendipitous art find.

'When you see it up close, unspoiled, it really is incredibly humbling,' he said. 'Splendidly vivid drawings, done all those thousands of years ago, but as if the artist were reaching out to you directly across the millennia. And considering that the chap who painted it was French, it makes it all the more remarkable what a decent job he's made of it. I only wish he were still alive to show the bloke who did our conservatory a trick or two.'

Right: With grateful thanks to Clyde McRoss of McRoss Damp Proofers for the loan of his 'Kango', without which the Museum would have been unable to source this particular section of the Meaux-Bottes cave wall.

5 Head Down Man

Human skull, Yorkshire grit
Grosmont visitor centre, 8000 BC

THESE MALE REMAINS were found on the North Yorkshire Moors by a hill-walker who had wandered far off trail in search of the so-called Bennett Beast, the surely apocryphal big cat that stalks the Moors and, in certain evening lights, resembles the popular local playwright. Our rambler may not have sighted a maternally preoccupied feral feline, but he found something with even more cultural significance for the proud county of Yorkshire: the skeleton of Head Down Man.

Wonderfully preserved in a mixture of peat and his own bile, Head Down Man lived in the Mesolithic Era. He was buried standing up but hunched over with a stone club in his hands; the fact that he was inhumed with it suggests that the implement was the primary tool of his trade. Palaeontologists nicknamed the finding Head Down Man because of the utterly determined way his 'face' seemed to be set and the resolute angle of the skull. Interestingly, although the club or bat was presumably greatly prized by the man, it rarely seems to have been used to hit anything in anger.

A multitude of notches on flat pieces of flint around the grave suggest that he was a great recorder and counter of whatever this trade might have been. The presence of some ball-shaped lumps of stone in the grave make it tempting to assume that Head Down Man was an early champion of Stone Age bat and ball games, but it is equally possible that his gifts may have been for oratory or wisdom, perhaps with the thousands of scratches denoting the number of times he had incanted the same observations.

Buried alongside him were some sticks of rhubarb and a primitive animal skin as worn by a Stone Age female for chores around the dwelling. Analogous to our modern apron or pinny, DNA testing suggests that it belonged to Head Down Man's grandmother.

6 Tutenkhamen's Tracksuit

Ancient Egyptian leisurewear
Thebes, 1324 BC

THIS EXQUISITE TRACKSUIT, found in 1927 on the so-called Mido expedition, was the burial garment of the young King Tutenkhamen and is the first and most significant item of sportswear we have from Ancient Egypt.

Tutenkhamen was a reactionary Pharaoh in many regards – he reversed his father Akhenaten's move towards monotheism in favour of a traditional polytheism and he banned cats – but he can defiantly lay claim to having been the first ruler in history to introduce organised keep-fit for all his subjects.

Under the personal supervision of the Pharaoh, all men and women were encouraged to perform vigorous exercises each morning, generally involving stretching, some resistance training and then carrying enormous lumps of limestone and alabaster until they dropped from exhaustion. Tutenkhamen took the fitness regime seriously: the penalty for slackers was 20 *bakh-hotep* – a sort of press-up – for the second offence, and death by impalement on spikes for the first. As the Egyptians 'worked out', prayers and incantations were offered to Lyc'Ra the Green Goddess, the deity associated with aerobic activity.

Judging from the skeleton, the young king was himself a fitness fanatic until he suffered a badly broken leg at the age of 18. A contemporary biographer-scribe insists that 'His Magnificence had trials for Crystal Palace but had to retire when he done his cruciate', although the veracity of this is questionable.

7 Calyxurea

Pottery, urine
Crete, precise date unknown

OF ALL THE TRAGEDIES and disillusionments begat by drug-cheating in sport, none has been more dispiriting than the revelations engendered by the 1874 discovery of this amphora. Found in Crete by olive thieves who handed it anonymously to the Knossos Adult Education Centre and Tzatziki Bar, it was a vessel for collecting and testing urine from athletes in the ancient world. Around its edges are the names of heroes under suspicion, the results of their samples and any subsequent bans from competition. Much of this was decoded in the 1890s by the English classicist and keen amateur urologist, Professor Dwain, who gives the amphora its name, the Dwain Chamberpot.

Professor Dwain contended that the most famous all-round athletic feat of them all was drug-assisted. According to the Professor's interpretation of records on the Dwain Chamberpot, Heracles accomplished his Twelve Labours while using performance-enhancing substances. After slaying the Nemean Lion, Heracles avoided a random sample, and missed a subsequent test after cleaning out the Aegean Stables in a time regarded as a suspicious improvement on previous efforts. By the time he actually failed a test retrieving the Belt of Hippolyta, a full-blown whispering campaign had started. Only by bullying his critics and threatening direct legal action by his father Zeus was Heracles able to keep competing, and he was eventually forced to hand back the apples of the Hesperides.

Professor Dwain claims that the scandal was hushed up, although his account should be taken with some caution given that he spent the second half of his life locked in an attic trying to distil urine from a bottle of olive oil he believed had belonged to Julius Caesar. He failed.

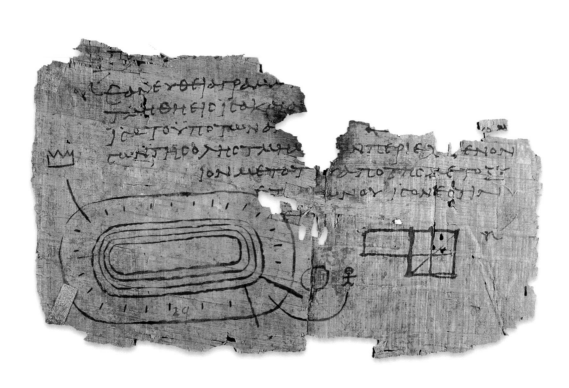

8 Stadium Design

Architectural sketch on papyrus
Ancient Greece, 853 BC

FROM THIS SCRAP of papyrus, found amid the rubble of a ruined temple on Mount Olympus, and a lesser-known translation of Homer by Boris Johnson, we can learn a little about the most remarkable sporting event of them all: the gathering of the Greek gods in the very first Olympic Stadium.

Unusually, Johnson translates Ζεύς, πατὴρ ἀνδρῶν τε θεῶν τε not as the standard 'Zeus, Father of Gods and Men' but 'Zeus, Mayor of Olympus'. In the Johnson interpretation, 'the crowning achievement of mighty Zeus is his helmsmanship of the original "Olympic Games"'.

The Johnson translation describes the logistical issues overcome by Zeus, from negotiating the awarding of refreshment concessions at the stadium (Nectar: official immortality drink of the Games), to a conflict over sponsorship rights with Athena Nike, and providing sufficient parking space for winged horses and fiery chariots. It would seem that some patrons attempted to bring in their own food or wine and were summarily dealt with by the organisers (death by thunderbolt), and that the Immortal Organising Committee put on an elaborate opening ceremony where the whole pantheon of gods and men of all races came together in a confusing and overlong festival of dance.

As to the stadium itself, we can piece together what we know from the Johnson text and ruins on Mount Olympus near Thessaloniki. It would appear that there was some controversy over unfilled seating, with banks upon banks left empty for members of the 'Olympus Family' and mere mortals forced to plead for entry in confusing and undignified circumstances.

9 Sponsored Toga

Marble bust, logograms
Jerusalem, 33 AD

THE CHARIOT RACE OF 33 AD, immortalised in *Ben-Hur*, very nearly never took place. It was the last scheduled contest in a chariot racing season that had been dogged by controversy from the start.

The first race in the calendar had seen the Taurus Redus team disqualified for producing a chariot with too much downward thrust, which lit the touch paper for an ill-tempered season. Race after race was marred by disagreements over what represented a fair design, with constant disputes between rival constructors, and attempts to bend the rules to their very limit. Eventually it was agreed to limit the horsepower of the chariots to one horse. However, this led to an unacceptable number of fatalities (zero) and, in a bid to satisfy the crowd's lust for blood, the safety chariot – hitherto used to string the competitors out after a crash – was dispensed with.

In the race prior to the Jerusalem Grand Prix in 33, a driver from Germania had been disqualified for attempting to run a competitor off the track. This in turn caused a protest from his powerful sponsors, who were already aggrieved at a ban on certain types of adverts on the side of chariots, notably those for sugared dormice and Christianity. That the race even went ahead was remarkable. That the Ben-Hur team's unusual strategy (one set of wheels, no spikes) proved a success was little short of a miracle.

10 Gladiatorial Mosaic

Small pieces of stone stuck to the floor
Pompeii, 59 AD

THIS IMPRESSIVE MOSAIC was found beneath the amphitheatre at Pompeii, on the floor of a room probably used as a changing area for gladiators. It served as both rudimentary informational conduit and clear warning of how things ought not to be done, much like the television programmes of my wildly overrated colleague Simon Schama.

It depicts an episode in 59 AD which saw a Pompeian *lanista* (trainer of gladiators), Deanus, caught instructing his men to fake injuries in the arena.

One of Deanus' men was fighting in the garb of the Harlequinista, a popular type of gladiator who wore brightly coloured quartered armour. On seeing his man's opponent, a fearsome Celt, Deanus realised that his fighter was doomed. He asked the *summa rudis* (referee) to allow a substitution, which was permissible if a gladiator was bleeding profusely from a previous encounter.

Deanus poured a bucket of cow's blood over the Harlequinista but sadly the guile of this plan did not match its boldness, as Deanus attempted this in full view of the thousands in the crowd. Panicking, Deanus ordered the attending medical and training staff (Medicus and Physius) to hack off the unfortunate gladiator's arm. Sadly, the nervous Medicus ended up decapitating the gladiator.

Some of the spectators were enraged by Deanus' painfully transparent attempts to cheat, while others regarded a severed head as being insufficient grounds for a gladiator to withdraw from combat. Either way, a riot broke out. Deanus was disgraced, and suspended from training gladiators for three years. The luckless Medicus was suspended, from a rope, in the entrance to the arena.

Left: This small section of floor has been kindly lent to the Museum under the EU Programme for Cultural Appropriations. A small section of carpet from the saloon bar of the Jolly Brewer, Westray, has been sent to the Museo Bolognese in exchange.

11 The Saint Murdoch Bible

Illuminated manuscript
Greater London, early 10th century

THIS EXQUISITELY ILLUSTRATED bible was found in 1992 in Isleworth, West London, but the circumstances of its discovery were far from edifying. A broadcast of *Antiques Roadshow* at nearby Syon House got out of hand and, egged on by Hugh Scully, members of the audience ran amuck in search of valuable Toby Jugs. Their looting spree reached as far as the Sky Television Broadcasting Headquarters in neighbouring Isleworth before police got the situation under control. One pensioner was apprehended by police, digging for booty with her bare hands in a raised bed at the back of the building. Yet out of this wanton criminality came a hugely important finding for sporting historians: she had unwittingly unearthed what came to be known as the Saint Murdoch Bible.

This bible appears to be from the 10th century, translated from the original Greek by Saint Murdoch. According to legend, he was the first person to import snakes into the British Isles. His bible differs from the King James version by supporting the belief that sport was intrinsic to humanity, indeed that it predated it. The fundamentalist Christian interpretation of the Saint Murdoch argues that mankind was specifically created by God *to* watch sport; that watching sport is not just a pastime or even a right, but our Christian duty.

Regrettably, there have been several recent attempts to call into question the provenance of the Manuscript. Some so-called experts have proffered evidence, via carbon-dating and the claim that the Saint Murdoch Bible was discovered inside a folder from Ryman, to argue that it was written in the present day. This theory is utterly discredited in serious academic circles.

Right: Folio 5. I am indebted to BSkyB for their loan of the manuscript and a most generous donation to the National Museum of the History of Sport, Orkney.

In the beginning God created the heaven and the earth. And the earth was without form, and void and darkness was upon the face of the deep. God said I shall create the Sky, and the Sports of the Sky, and the games that are played with the foot. Thus he created them, and footballers did he form out of clay, and from their rib he fashioned Woman to read out the Sky Sports News Headlines and he set Adam to watch it while Eve toiled under the burdens of her Sin. And God saw that this made much money, and he saw that it was good. And on the Seventh Day he rested and watched Sky Super Sunday.

12 The Dubai Codex

Vegetable dyes on Rolodex-codex
Yúcatan, 1044

THIS INTRIGUING LITTLE TREASURE was appropriated from an unknown Mayan city by a 16th-century Conquistador called El Haroon. On his voyage back to the Old World, El Haroon was in his turn relieved of it by an English seafarer – a pirate, to all intents and purposes – Lord Giles. It has enjoyed a chequered history of sale, theft and disappearance ever since. Today it resides in the headquarters of the ICC; hence it is often referred to as the Dubai Codex.

Mayan scholars believe that the Dubai Codex lays out, in painstaking detail, the international cricket calendar and the Future Tours Programme. Deciphering the hieroglyphs and tallying cricket's history with the Mesoamerican Long Count calendar used by the Maya, events from cricket's past and present fixture list (the granting of Test status to Sri Lanka in 1981, Bradman's 1948 Invincibles playing every County, Virginia Woolf's 1926 appearance for Gentlemen v Players in a false beard) are detailed with astonishing accuracy.

A careful reading of the Codex allowed the ICC to plan cricketing fixtures until very recently, and the wisdom of antiquity proved invaluable when trying to fit as many ODI tournaments as possible into any given year. However, there was widespread concern that the relic was predicting the end of the world in 2012, as it appeared to cease detailing cricket matches after December that year. Fortunately, scholars now believe that this was in fact a reference to the rebranding of the Friends Provident as the Clydesdale Bank Pro 40, with the confusion down to a small illegible portion on the face of the Codex.[1]

---

1 Thought to have been damaged by former England captain Mike Gatting when he was invited to inspect the Codex during a 1987 ceremony to unveil a new display, DNA testing suggests the smear is consistent with HP sauce from a sausage sandwich.

13 The Lakeside Tapestry
Frimley Green, 1066

THIS MAGNIFICENT WORK of embroidery, 230 feet long, depicts in painstaking detail one of the most bitter and significant conflicts in British sporting history: the 11th-century defeat of indigenous Saxon darts players by the Normans.

Darts had been played in these Isles since post-Roman times in a form almost identical to today's game, the only differences being the invention of the Tungsten barrel and that players in previous eras drank mead rather than today's lager.

The native Briton *darters ordinary* were unprepared for the invasion of the better organised invaders who, their enormous guts barely constrained by their shiny smocks, presented a dazzling, intimidating sight on the oche as they threw their lethal darts. Their best troops, the *Princes de Chevaliers* were an especially fearsome

unit, led by Sieur Erique De Bristeau. After the invaders cut a swathe through the South of England, winning a series of exhibition skirmishes in pubs and inns, the British *darters ordinary*, who had been drinking heavily overnight to steady their nerves, staggered out to meet them at Frimley in what would become the Battle of Lakeside.

The native forces fought bravely under their beloved leader Bob of George, but were no match for the sheer alcoholic capacity and accuracy under extreme intoxication of the invading PDC. While rousing his men in a cry of 'God for England, Bobby and St George' and refilling a tankard of ale, Bob was felled by an accurate treble assault that scored an unfortunate bull's-eye. The killer blow was apocryphally thrown by De Bristeau himself, but historians think it more likely that a Scottish mercenary by the name of Jock Wilsonne may have dealt the fatal dart.

le Secconde Noue   sfera del Diauolo

14 The Back Nine Circles of Hell

Satanic golf course design
Florence, 1313

DID DANTE ALIGHIERI have a nightmarish vision of the first unplayable golf course?

That is the contention of a new book entitled *The Divine Comedy: Pitching Wedge out of Purgatory* by Dr Miles Foutaize, Professor of Golf History and Difficult Poetry at the Sorbonne. Dr Foutaize suggests that Dante learned about a golf-type game being played in the Netherlands around the late 13th century and that the imagination of the great Florentine poet was captured by the maddening sport. It is probable that the well-travelled Dante was one of the first wealthy Europeans to play golf around the continent: there are records of him visiting Edinburgh and St Andrews around 1301 and also a diary account of a trip to the Algarve.

And it further seems that the new sport of golf influenced Dante's vision for his masterpiece, *The Divine Comedy*. According to Dr Foutaize, Dante may have envisioned his journey through the nine Circles of Hell as an allegory for a particularly challenging golf course. In the Foutaize reading, the condemned souls arranged in the concentric circles are in torment not for the deadly sins of lust, gluttony, etc but rather of breaches of golf club etiquette. In this illustration opposite, demons await on the outer circle for those who have played a ball from an incorrect lie. The next six circles denote progressively more horrific heavy rough and water hazards. Further towards the centre there is a black hole, the eternal fate of those wretches who had marked a scorecard incorrectly.

At the very centre, Satan himself waits to torture and torment those who had committed what Dante identified as the greatest sin of all: wearing waterproof outerwear in the clubhouse. Their fate, involving Satan and a sharpened golf tee, was truly gruesome, and, as Dante noted, 'it served them right, as per club rule 24.7 (c), which is clearly visible on the celestial noticeboard.'

15 Votive Offering

Golden man on raft
Inca Peru, 1320

THIS STATUE WAS recovered from Lake Huaypo, a few miles
north-west of the McDonald's a few miles north-west of historic
Cusco in Peru, and depicts an early rower. Records from Spanish
conquistadors suggest that rowing races were a popular pastime
for the elite in pre-Columbian Inca society. The highlight was
an annual contest between the young clerics of two noted tribes,
although some accounts suggest that both sides attempted to gain
unfair advantage by importing older, stronger oarsmen from the
Northern Americas.

This little gold token would have been thrown into the lake as
a votive offering to curry favour with the Inca god of rowing and
competition, Redgravu. In addition, it may have been used as a
projectile weapon. Evidence suggests that members of the lower
orders attempted to protest these rowing contests of the privileged by
getting in the water and upending the boats. The rowers sometimes
threw small but heavy gold trinkets at them in retaliation, or made
deafening braying noises to scare them off.

Right: This statue appears to have some sort of (partially damaged) head-dress, perhaps a
denoter of academic achievement, although it may be that the vertical object on the left side
of the head is in fact a primitive snorkel. It is possible that members of the rowing teams
jumped out of their boats in order to engage protestors *mano-a-mano submarino*, although a
large piranha population suggests that underwater fisticuffs may have been a dubious tactic
for both factions.

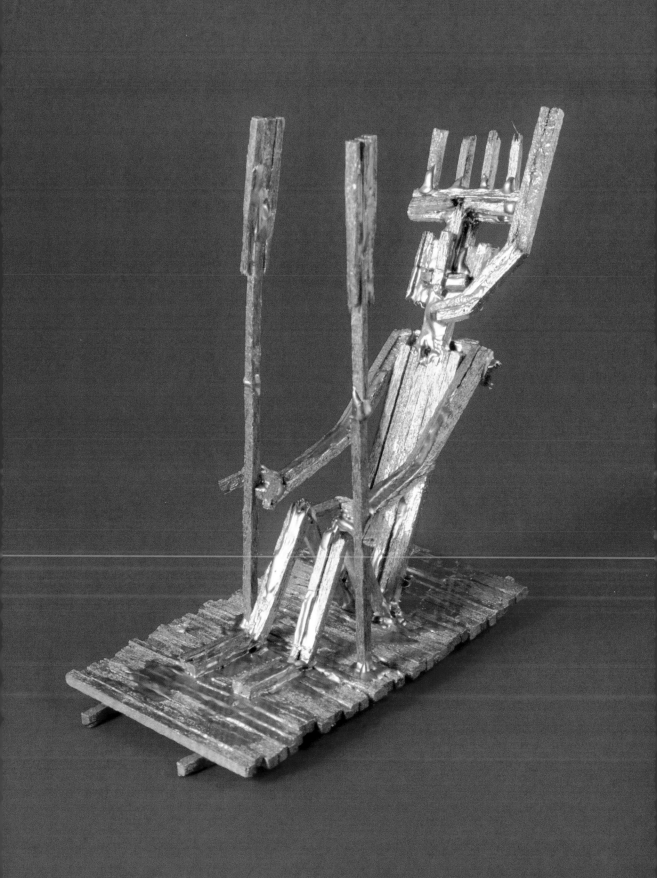

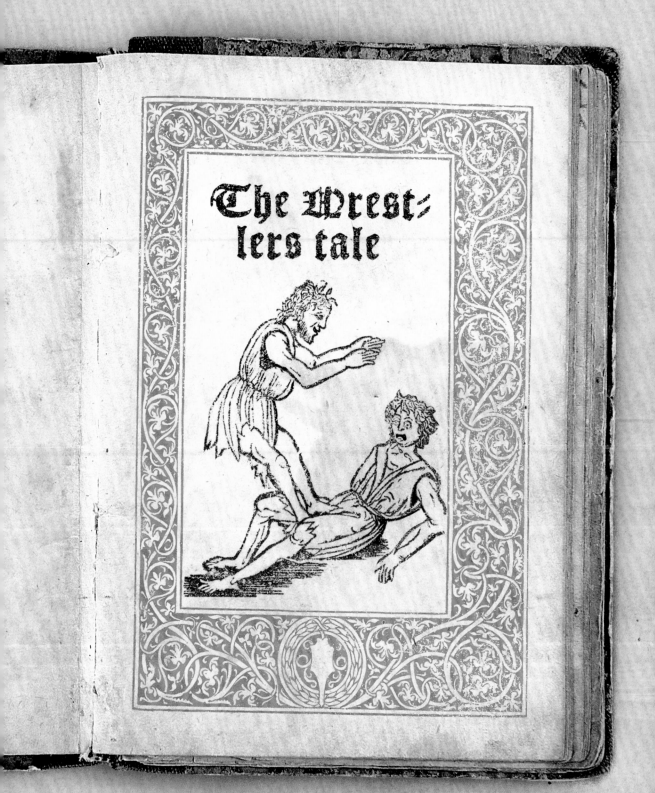

16 The Wrestler's Tale

Early English poetry
Canterbury, 1392

IT HAD LONG vexed sporting historians that one of the great early works of the English language had scant reference to sport. Imagine, then, the joy in our little community when an early edition of Chaucer's *Canterbury Tales* was found in the ruins of a priory in Sandwich, containing a previously undiscovered section.

The Wrestler's Tale opens with the character beginning 'introduced' to his fellow pilgrims by the Wife of Bath, who notes approvingly:

> *A righte huge fellowe got then to his feete*
> *His bodye was bigge, his trunkes were tiny*
> *His mightye armes were as great slabbes of meate*
> *And his hairye was long and fayre and shiny*

The Wrestler's Tale largely consists of insults directed at an opponent or rival – 'Trashe Talkynge' being an important facet of the brutal wrestling bouts in Chaucer's time. The opponent addressed here seemingly had some other employment beyond grappling, perhaps as an embalmer or gravedigger.

> *Is thou listenynge to me Undertaykere?*
> *Indeede I am goinge to whippe your erse*
> *Thou art trulee runnynge scared of mye powere*
> *I wylle beate you lyke as I beate Jake Ye Snake*
> *And Rowdy Sir Rodericke the Pyper*
> *Ande all other fooles who dare me challenge*
> *I wylle crushe thee as thou arte a flye*
> *What do ye saye to thatte, you bytche?*

The Wrestler does not travel with the pilgrims long, probably going off to fight this Undertaykere for a purse, and leaves after being accused by the Pardoner of taking money under false pretences. It seems the wrestling bouts of the day were fixed; and by the time of the 15th century, wrestling was generally regarded as a branch of the entertainment industry rather than the fine manly pursuit of today.

17–19 Prophetic Tarot Cards

Woodcuts on paper
Provence, France, 1530

WHILE THE PROPHESIES of Nostradamus on politics and great social events are very famous, it is less well known that the apothecary-soothsayer was also keenly interested in sports.

As a young man growing up in Provence, he first attempted to see into the future to predict dog races. Always looking to broaden his areas of clairvoyant expertise, and income, he set up in Avignon what could regarded as the first 'tipster' service. For a fee, a citizen could enter a booth and, from behind a curtain, Nostradamus would dispense his prophecies, charging a coin a minute and two a minute during peak times.

His skill in predicting the results of boules, competitive pâté-eating and mistress-racing saw his fame grow. Soon the crowned heads of Europe were seeking out Nostradamus for predictions on jousting, hunting wagers and even an early version of *It's a Royal Knockout* in which he foresaw which royal spouses would be beheaded in the future.

However, Nostradamus found himself out of luck in 1558 when he erroneously advised Emperor Ferdinand I to wager an enormous sum on a cockfight that went sideways. He was forced to flee Avignon in such a hurry that he had no time to gather up his collection of writings on sport, which remained undiscovered for centuries. Some of the most astonishly prescient are gathered here.

XIIII

LE·CHEVALIER

In the land of the red headed men shall rise
A creature of great and terrible power
No fence will tame him nor ditch him contain
And he shall be available at 33/1 in Ladbrokes

Above: Thought to be a prophecy suggesting that the locally trained Bongo's Jetpack would win the 1985 Scottish Grand National. In fact, he fell at the first and the race was won by Fiddling Keith. However, the Ayrshire stables where Bongo's Jetpack was housed did later burn down in what court reports identified as 'a clear case of insurance fraud'. This has been cited by Nostradamus scholars as being an alternative reinterpretation of the 'great and terrible power' referred to.

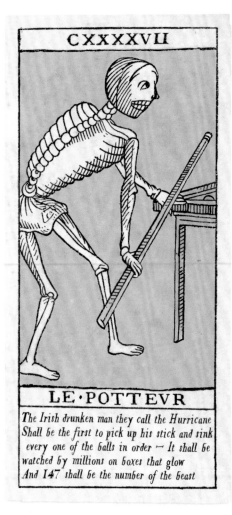

CXXXXVII

LE · POTTEVR

The Irish drunken man they call the Hurricane
Shall be the first to pick up his stick and sink
every one of the balls in order — It shall be
watched by millions on boxes that glow
And 147 shall be the number of the beast

VI

LE · CHANCEVX

A man or woman shall rise up from humble birth
Or possibly from a family of great wealth
Mighty or disappointing will be his or her feats
And there shall be considerable rejoicing,
or sadness

Left: This prediction comes from the recently discovered *Snookerus Predictamus* volume that Nostradamus composed during a 1524 visit to Sheffield. 'The Irish drunken man they call the Hurricane' is most probably Alex Higgins, and the event referred to is obviously the first televised ('watched on boxes') maximum break in snooker. In fact, this was accomplished not by Higgins, but by Steve Davis, in the quarter-finals of the 1982 Lada Classic, so this is probably a mistranslation from the original French: 'Irish drunken man' could alternatively be interpreted to be 'thin quiet man from Essex' while there are similarities in 16th-century French spellings of 'The Hurricane' and 'Steve "The Nugget" Davis'.

Right: Perhaps the most remarkably farsighted of all Nostradamus' sporting prophesies, there can be little doubt that this refers to Luton Town gaffer Ray Harford, who managed the Hatters to an unlikely League Cup triumph over Arsenal at Wembley in 1988. The victory hinged on the late penalty save by Andy Dibble ('a man or woman' from 'humble birth or possibly a family of great wealth'). The kick had been taken by Nigel Winterburn ('disappointing').

20 Royal Box
Hampton Court, 1535

HENRY VIII wore this abdominal protector for jousting, fencing and executing his wives. Increasingly unreasonable with age, the king refused to change his codpiece for months at a time; contemporary accounts report him boasting of spending 'the whole of the yeare of Our Lord 1530 with ye crowne jewelles tucked away sayfe in mye boxe for all seasons'. This fanatical guarding of his genitals was almost certainly due to the king's desperate desire for a male heir and his rising paranoia that spies of the Papacy might attempt to have a rummage through the royal undergarments.

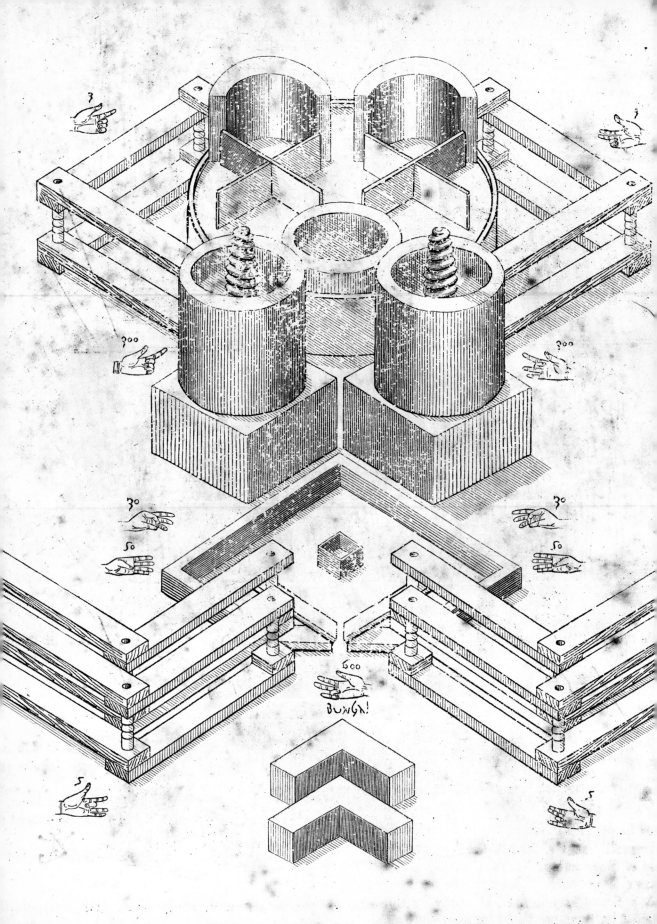

BUNGA!

21 Bunga Bunga Court

Design for Italian Renaissance ball game
Milan, 1590

FROM THE JOURNAL of an Ambrosian monk in Lombardy in the 16th century, we have a vivid account of one of the first codified ball-and-hand sports in Southern Europe. A Friar Silvio describes in gloriously passionate detail the rules of Bunga Bunga, which was played by himself and other monks up against the wall of a chapel. Some of the exact terminology remains obscure, murky in antiquity, but the Rossoneri (1606) translation reprinted here is widely accepted in academic circles. Friar Silvio wrote:

> After the Sacrement on Tuesday I hurried round to the back of the chapel for a game of Bunga Bunga. I have managed to get my hands on a Nun[1] and give her a good spank on the bottom,[2] shouting 'Fruity! Fruity!'[3] as I did so before the Cardinal[4] caught me. I was declared the winner and went off to speak to my legal team[5] in order to prove that I had never seen that nun before in my life.[6]

---

1 *Nun* was probably the term used in Bunga Bunga for the ball.

2 The object in Bunga Bunga was to bounce the *Nun* on the back wall (the *bottom*). A *good spank* was probably slang for a well-executed shot.

3 Friar Silvio was an irrepressible character who played Bunga Bunga in a state of near-religious ecstasy. The cry of 'Fruity! Fruity!' was traditional if a player made a particularly well-struck shot.

4 The Cardinal was almost certainly the referee or umpire, responsible for timekeeping.

5 'Speak to my legal team' is a reference to praying to God.

6 Friar Silvio, a brilliant Bunga Bungista, would most likely have wanted to keep his exact techniques and tactics secret from other players.

22 The 'Flying Franc'

Gold coin
Chateau de Toujours-Piste-Oeuf, France, 1643

No sporting visionary has been more ambitious, more determined or more utterly hopeless than the 17th-century French monarch Edouard, The Snow King. Convinced of his divine right to soar through the air, Edouard the Eagle spent unimaginable fortunes creating an elaborate series of ramps, jumps and propelling devices at the Palais des Tuileries.

As a young boy, Edouard had seen his father Louis the Bastard and his uncle, Louis the Total Bastard, push a beloved nanny off the roof of the palace, shouting 'fly, fly, my pretty'. The trauma, and the zeal to fly, informed his entire adult life. He engaged the finest inventors in Europe, prayed devoutly and reportedly dabbled with witchcraft as he attempted to propel himself further and further through the air. He had little aptitude for it.

Early leaps taught the King the sobering lesson that, while the Royal mind might be touching the heavens, the Royal body remained sadly earthbound and indeed more fragile than he would have liked. Edouard thus instructed his head chef to whip up tens of thousands of egg whites and decorate his workshop, creating soft, cushiony meringues to make his inevitable crash landings somewhat more bearable.

The sight of the Snow King soaring (albeit briefly) through the air is captured here in this coin, which understandably does not show the result of the endeavour, to wit the king coming a cropper in a bed of pudding. The monarch's behaviour became something of a national embarrassment, and while his cause of death aged 47 was officially recorded as 'pox', it is probable that Edouard the Eagle's goggles steamed up during a flight and that he fractured his skull mistaking a harpsichord for the more forgiving landing area of a giant crème caramel.

Left: On loan from the Pimlico Coinarium, a wonderful gallimaufry of antique coins assembled by Nicholas Astbury-What, Professor of Pocket Shrapnel at the New York Numismatic Institute for Achievement in Excellence.

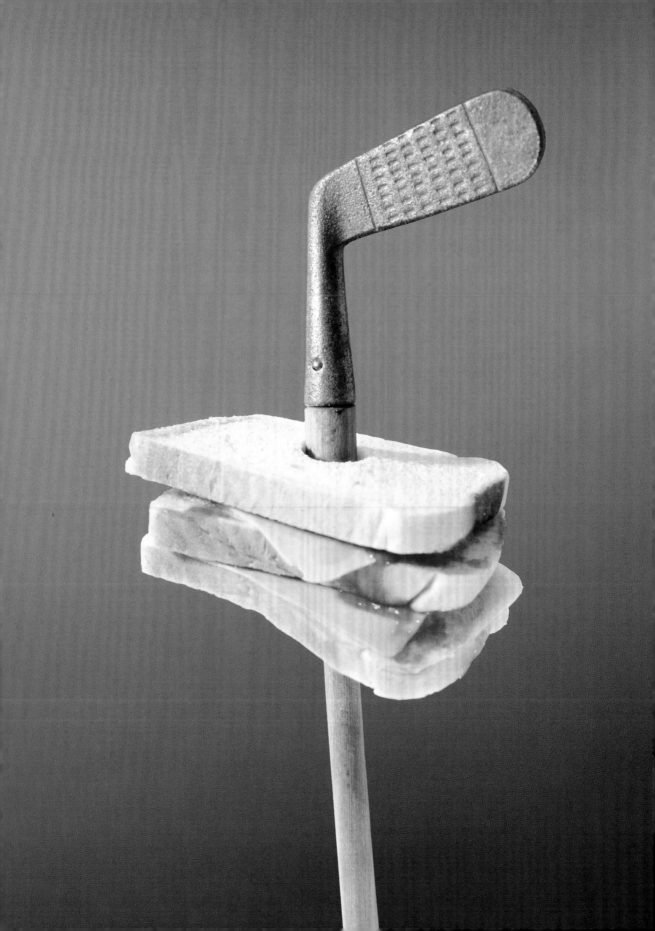

23 Sand Wedge

Hickory, iron, ketchup
St Andrews, 1763

FROM THE DIARY of Sandy 'Bloomers' Montgomerie, a caddy at the St Andrews golf club, comes this description of a development in golf technology made by John Montagu, Fourth Earl of Sandwich, First Lord of the Admiralty and second-rate golfer:

It was a perfect July day at St Andrews but as we strode down the first fairway with the horizontal sleet in our faces, I was concerned.

His Lordship had lunched well, although he had neglected to eat any food. When we saw his ball in a spiteful sand-trap, my heart sank. His Lordship was prone to fits of temper when ensnared in a bunker, especially when ahungered. He howled at me fit to unsettle the horses from Troon to Aberdeen.

'Lyle! Torrance! Whatever your damn fool name is.'

'Montgomerie, your Lordship,' I murmured. 'A tricky lie there and no mistake.'

'Sandwich!' he bellowed. 'Bring me a sandwich.'

I made quickly to the bag and began hastily assembling an emergency repast of cold meats between two slices of bread. I presented it to his Lordship, hoping this would avert further unpleasantness.

'You Scotch oaf,' he roared. 'I want a sand wedge, not a sandwich.'

I ran to fetch the most forgiving iron in our arsenal, a flat niblick ideal for hacking out of just such a bunker. His Lordship threw the meaty snack after me. With uncharacteristic accuracy, it hit me on the head.

My last memory – as his lordship battered me about the head and neck with his short iron and bits of meat dripped down my back – was of the other gentlemen chortling and shouting 'Now that is what I call a club sandwich.'

I never set foot on a golf course again.

Left: This club is an original iron from a set owned by Sandy Montgomerie; the sandwich is a modern reconstruction.

24 Beaver Totem

Wood, fur, mainly teeth
Uruguay, 1780

ONLY FOUND ACROSS the Steppes and in North America today, the beaver had an extinct cousin: the Uruguayan or biting beaver (*beaveris chompis*). It was a remarkable creature, the only one of the rodent family documented as playing in social groups for amusement's sake.

On a 1780 botanical and golf trip to South America, the Scottish explorer Kenneth Mathieson observed Uruguayan beavers masticating tree bark into a ball shape and flicking it to each other with their paws.

'I have watched the Uruguayan beavers playing together on top of one of their dams, each taking turns to push a ball of chewed-up wood towards the other, seemingly delighting in the game,' Mathieson wrote. 'However, it seems to be in the nature of the creature to spoil this charming scene: after just a few minutes, one of the beavers dived off the log and onto the floor and made heart-rending sounds as if injured, although I could see nothing the matter with it. It then attempted to bite one of its fellows for no reason and without provocation and, upon seeing a rival of very dark pelt, began spitting and hissing at it in a most unpleasant manner.'

Despite its unattractive behaviour, the beaver was fiercely venerated by tribal natives, who went to great lengths to defend it from outside aggressors. Judging from one or two surviving, weather-beaten totem poles – such as this one pictured left – the beaver was even worshipped. But Mathieson's account made the animal a must-have specimen for European naturalists and, sadly, for hunters as well. It was extinct within two generations of discovery.

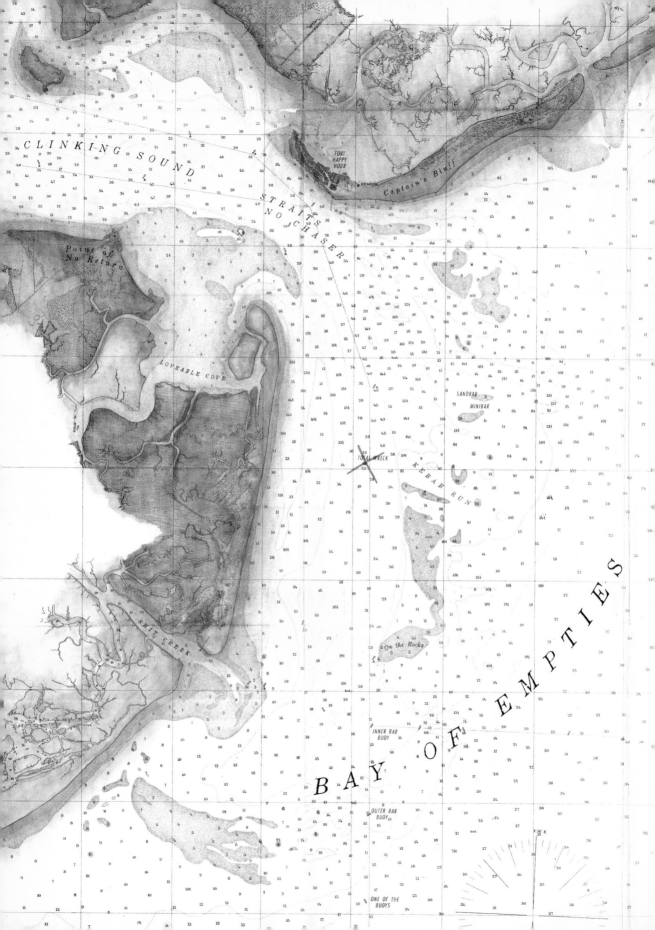

CLINKING SOUND

STRATH CHASER NO

Point of
No Return

Captain's Bluff

FORT
HAPPY
HOUR

BEACON

LOVEABLE COVE

SANDBAR
MINIBAR

KEBAB RUN

TOTAL WRECK

On the Rocks

SHIT CREEK

B A Y   O F   E M P T I E S

INNER BAR
BUOY

OUTER BAR
BUOY

ONE OF THE
BUOYS

25 Original Pirate Material

Nautical chart, traces of Banana Daiquiri
St Lucia, 1801

THIS CHART SHOWS the suspected position of one of British seafaring's most spectacular wrecks. The HMS Fredalo, commanded by a Captain Andrew, sunk in the Caribbean Sea at the end of the 18th century and immediately became a source of horrified fascination for the naval establishment.

It was believed that Captain Andrew had taken on board a cargo of some 6,000 cases of Bacardi, which he then took on board his person in a heroic display of carousing. Contemporary accounts suggest that he was well onto his 14,000th bottle when he handed control of the vessel to his First Mate, Worharmy. Unfortunately, the trusted lieutenant panicked and steered the ship miles off course, running her aground on the Second Slips and consigning her to a watery grave.

Captain Andrew and some of his crew made it to shore, but the wreck caused a major environmental disaster in the region, with local marine life severely inebriated for generations to come. The disgraced Captain Andrew became a prize fighter and vaudeville act, while First Mate Worharmy retired to the North East to spend more time with his beard.

26 Fairy Tale

Woodcutter woodcut on paper
Enchanted Forest, Germany, 1821

ONE OF THE LESS well-known of the fairy tales by the brothers Grimm, *Die Eisprinzessin* (*The Ice Princess*) was a cautionary fable about the dangers of unfettered competitiveness, jealousy and inappropriately short sequined dresses. Growing up in Steinau an der Straße, the brothers were keen ice skaters and won the under-11 boys' (not suitable for children) pairs section of a prestigious regional skating contest. It is surely from here that they drew their inspiration for their notably horrifying children's bedtime story, *Die Eisprinzessin*. Here is a translated extract:

> The Ice King was wise and greatly loved his two daughters. Princess Nancy was beautiful and good but the other daughter, Princess Tonya, was evil and jealous. The King organised a contest where the two princesses would dance on the frozen lake and whichever one danced the most beautifully would be wed to a handsome prince and showered with gold. Princess Nancy practised day and night at her skating but, tricked by wickedness and thoughts of gold, some woodcutters and ruffians attacked poor Princess Nancy. They tried to turn her into a swan but could not remember the correct spell so they hit her in the leg with an iron bar. The bad men were soon captured and taken to the dungeon. Princess Tonya said that she had not known about the plan, even though nobody could think of any other reason why the woodcutters would attack Princess Nancy. The people of the land called Princess Tonya a monster and she was turned into a toad so that all the people could point at her and they all lived happily ever after. The end.

27–28 Leather Tankards

Cocktail boots
Warwickshire, 1823

As EVERY SCHOOLBOY knows, William Webb Ellis achieved sporting immortality at Rugby School in 1823 when he picked up a football boot with his hands and drank ale out of it, thus inventing rugby players.

These boots were found in an attic at the public school with a handwritten essay from Webb Ellis detailing the exact formula for a post-match celebration cocktail that should be drunk out of them. Sadly, the only words that are legible are 'beer … prop's vomit' and what appears to say 'jockstrap juice (not gay)' but the rest of the recipe has been obscured in its entirety due to the scrawling of the lyrics to 'Four And Twenty Virgins' across it.

While the boots themselves are Webb Ellis's original pair, it is likely that the cocktail umbrella dates from a later time, probably the mid-19th century.

29 Australian Rules Uniform Pattern

Cloth, ink, Aussie spunk
Melbourne, 1859

EDITOR's NOTE: I am indebted to Professor Merv MacGregor, Chair of Ancient History at the New South Wales University of Sport, Narromine, for the loan of this original illustration of an early Australian Rules Football uniform and his acclaimed thesis upon it.

In stark contrast to the shameful underfunding of academic sports history in the UK, in Australia our subject enjoys an equal status to such core curriculum disciplines as creative outdoor linguistics, competitive mathematics and applied sexism. Professor MacGregor presides over a magnificent £100m state-of-the-art faculty which has a dedicated carbon-dating laboratory, archival space twice that of the British Museum, and its own sheep dip. It goes without saying that the quality of research produced by his institution is world class.

This drawing shows an 1859 match between the South Melbourne Shanes and the North Victoria Men at Work and was used as a blueprint for early Australian Rules uniforms. I am delighted to reproduce Professor MacGregor's brilliant paper on the subject in its entirety.

Professor Merv MacGregor:

> The vest was probably sewn by this bloke's sheila and that hat is a fair dinkum beaut, the very first Baggy Green worn by an Aussie, back in the day when all Australian hats were made of iron though so it was called an Iron Green. It makes you bloody proud. That roo looks like a hell of a competitor.

ATTEMPTED MURDER AND SUICIDE.

man named Caroline Smith was brought before
nty bench at Wokingham (Berks) on Tuesday,
with attempting to commit self-murder by stran-
and drowning, in the parish of Hurst, on the
Friday.

pears that the woman is married, and resides in
-court, Reading. She is well known in the parish
t, and was seen on the afternoon of Friday under
's-bridge, where she was evidently endeavouring
wn herself in a stream not much over her knees.
discovered she was brought out of the water,
thick piece of tape was found to be tied very
round her neck, which was cut with some diffi-
and a deep impression was found to have been
y the tape. She talked very incoherently to the
s who took her out of the water, and accused her
having two days before attempted to strangle her
aged seven years, but he was too strong for her.
iry the police found the statement to be true.
first remand she repeated her attempt at suicide,
ile in Reading gaol she made another attempt.
s committed for trial.

KILLED IN THE STREET.

uesday afternoon Mr. William Payne, the coroner
don and Southwark, held an inquiry at Guy's Hos-
especting the death of Charles William Smith, aged
even years.

deceased, it appears, was the son of a police-con-
On the afternoon of the 13th inst., he was play-
Thornton-street, Horselydown, Bermondsey, and
n the act of running across the road he slipped and
his face at the time a horse and waggon, heavily
with sacks of potatoes, came along, and before the
nate could get up the near wheel of the vehicle
over his body. He was picked up and taken to
Hospital, where it was found that his hip-bone was
ed and severely lacerated, from the effects of which
red on Saturday evening last. No blame attached
driver, and the Jury returned a verdict of "Acci-
death."

ANOTHER ANIMAL HORROR.

Savannah Advertiser reports another monster of
imal creation. It narrates that "a party," coming
annah from South Carolina, through Wright River,
morning of the 28th ult., towards noon, was,
is negro men, pulling quietly along near shore,
the slight-built craft was suddenly lifted up, as
ne immense roller, throwing the crew out of their
and completely scaring the life out of them."
ock was so sudden that there was some danger
boat turning over; but luckily it righted again,
ak back into the foaming water. The reason of
ock is thus graphically described by "the party,"
ys:—"I did not heed the danger around me, nor
ling fear of the men with me, for I could not, if
as at stake, have taken my eyes away from the
is creature that had caused all the commotion and
aking its way lazily out of the river into the long
s on the bank. Never before had I anticipated
monstrosity, nor do I ever wish to see another. A
re almost indescribable, though its general appear-
fixed in my mind's eye too indelibly for pleasant
hought. The beast, fish, or reptile, whatever
s of God's creation it might be classed under, was
awny greenish colour, growing more definite towards
ead. The body of the creature was seal-shaped, ap-
tly twenty feet long, and as thick as the carcass of
argest-sized elephant. From this trunk sprang
the most remarkable feature of the phenomenon—
curved swan-like neck, large enough apparently to
aken a man in whole, terminated by a head and jaws
r to that of an immense boa constrictor, the eyes
yet possessing ferocity enough in their expression
ike a man tremble. The back of the beast was
ridged, the ridges running from the base of the
to the extreme end of the tail, and several inches
An immense tail, shaped like an alligator's, and
times longer, so it seemed, than the body, completed
ut ensemble of this wonderful anomaly. The crea-
navigated by feet, resembling the forefeet of an
tor, and its progress on land was slow. With all this
ination of the terrible before me it was not strange
trembled; but before the frightened men had time
or I time to advise, the cause of our terror drew
across the little island out of sight into the water
d."

e WARWICK MURDERER.—Thomas Chapman, who
committed by the Warwick Borough magistrates,
nce his incarceration in Warwick Gaol, showed a great
nt of depression as to the awful situation in which
placed. Although his self-possession still remains,
hen alone in his cell, apparently in deep thought

THE LIFE, TRIAL, AND EXECUTION OF FREDERICK
BAKER.
With several Illustrations, Correct View of the Execution.
Portrait of the Murderer, Portrait of the Victim, &c.
Forming a complete account of the Incidents in connection with

THE ALTON MURDER.
THE MURDERER'S CONFESSION.
Comprised in 20 8vo. pages. ONE PENNY, POST TWOPENCE.
G. PURKESS, 286, Strand.

IMPERIAL AUSTRIAN GUARANTEED
STATE LOANS. No Lotteries. Bonâ-fide chances to win
for £1 the large premiums of
£30,000, £25,000, £20,000, &c., &c.
Public drawings on the First of every Month, under the super-
intendence of the Austrian Government; and official public
functionaries. Official Lists sent Gratis to Subscribers. Apply
for £1 chances, issued upon forms supplied by the Austrian
Government and bearing the Imperial half a florin stamp, and
for prospectuses to VOELCKER & CO., Bankers, Vienna.

JAQUES'S CROQUET (two prize medals, 1862).
Prices, including all the latest improvements, from 15s.
per set. Descriptive list on application—Sold by all dealers.
Wholesale, JAQUES and SON, 102, Hatton-garden. Caution.—To
guard against imitations observe the name "Jaques and Son"
on each box.

MERCHANT SEAMENS' ORPHAN ASYLUM,
Snaresbrook, E.—The Secretary begs to ACKNOW-
LEDGE, with thanks, the RECEIPT of £15, contributed to
the funds of the Institution by the passengers, officers, and crew
of the Peninsular and Oriental Company's Steamship, Colum-
bian, per favour Capt. G. Hyde.
117 and 118, Leadenhall-street, April 26, 1876.

WONDERFUL FOOTBALL DISCOVERY.
Showing the true cases of Nervous, Mental, Physical
Debility, Lowness of Spirits, Relegation, WANT OF ENERGY,
PREMATURE DECLINE, with plain directions for PERFECT
PASSING and VIGOUROUS TACKLING, properly directed.

THE TRANSFERIC TELEGRAPHON!
NOW WITH ADDED HEARSAY

286, STRAND.

TO LADIES.—Dr. Ralph Richardson can be
confidently consulted daily (as usual) in all diseases
Letters answered. Medicines sent. 101, Drury lane, London.

ONE PACKET ONLY OF PROF. VARLEY'S
GENERATIVE POWDERS is warranted to cure (in
either sex) the worst cases of Nervous Debility, Weakness. The
increasing demand for these Powders, through the recommenda-
tions of restored patients, unquestionably prove their astonishing efficacy for the Debilitated. Post free, 60 stamps. Address,
Prof. VARLEY, Vaughan-terrace, Maindee, Newport, Mon.

THE FUTURE FORETOLD.

THE RETURN OF MADAME DE VERE TO
ENGLAND—The ladies of England are informed that
Madame de Vere will reveal by clairvoyance, second sight, and
perception, the thoughts and intentions of others in any part of
THE WORLD. Four questions answered for thirteen stamps.
Address—Silvertown, London, E.

TO THE LADIES OF GREAT BRITAIN.—
The School of Physiology is now established by Dr.
Bruce, from Chicago, U.S., and conducted by Mrs. Dr. Bruce.
Every parent in America has his daughters taught this Science
before they are eighteen years of age. Pamphlets on Dr. Bruce's
inventions and catalogues of Physiological books (fit for any
lady to read) sent for 8 stamps by Dr. BRUCE, Dorking, Surrey.
Those in doubtful health should write.

A GENTLEMAN having been cured of the results of youthful error will be happy to send a copy
of the prescription used, on receipt of two stamps, for ex-
penses in transmission.—Address, MEDICUS, 365, Lower Ken-
nington-road, London.

RESPECTABLE PERSONS WHO WANT TO INCREASE THEIR

With three large Illustrations, Prese
showing the process of being made "Beau
Sixteen pages of Letterpress, Portraits,
G. PURKESS, 286, Strand.

TODMORDEN MURDE

Now Ready, One Penny, Post Twopence, the
Execution of
MILES WETHERI
With Interesting Particulars—Letters fro
never before published—Eight Illustrations—C
the Murderer and his Sweetheart—View of the
Murder of Jane Smith—The Attack on the Re
with Full and Correct View of the Execution
8vo. pages
G. PURKESS, 286, Strand.

ARISTOTLE! ARIS
The only Authentic Edition of this Extr
containing 400 pages, beautiful coloured plate
somely bound, sent by post only, carefully
address, on receipt of 48 stamps.
N.B.—Beware of Spurious Imitat
London: W. FORD, 3, Johnson's-court, Fle

Just published, sent by post only on receipt o

ARISTOTLE'S MASTERPIECE;
of Nature fully explained. Invaluable t
and after marriage.
London: W. EYRE, 31, Fetter-lane.

Now ready, by post only, on receipt of 40 p

THE FORBIDDEN
London: EDWIN LLOYD, 16, Shoe-lane, F

METHRALTON, THE GREAT
reveal your future. Seven years, six
twelve stamps. State age. Charm for Love, &
Methralton's Bible Key, 2s. 2d. Book of Spirits
bound, 4s. 2d. Dream Book, 3ss. 2d., stamp
Post-office, Daventry.

Just ready, a New Edition, cloth, gilt edges,
Thirteen Stamps.

A DICTIONARY OF LOVE;
contained the Explanation of most of t
the Love Language.
London: ALFRED T. CROCKER, 303 and

WONDERS of the HOROSCOP
son sending an addressed envelo
colour of hair and eyes, together with 13 sta
within 24 hours a correct likeness of their
wife, and date of marriage.—Address, A. W
street, Red Lion-square, London.

WHISKERS! MOUSTACHI
BROWS! guaranteed in a few weeks
of hair on bald patches, scanty partings, &c.
addressed envelope to Mr. LATREILLE, 99,
Walworth, Surrey.

YOUR FUTURE FORETOLD
wishing to have their future revealed
should send their age, sex, and thirteen sta
20, Whitfield-street, Tottenham-court-road. L

OVID'S ART OF LOVE, 1s.
Masterpiece, coloured plates, 2s. 6d.; M
1s.; Mysteries of a Convent, 2s.; Lewis's Mor
Lists of facetious works sent on receipt
WARREN, Potter's Bar, London, N.

GIVEN AWAY TO NERVOUS
20,000 copies of the "Warning Voice,"
Friend," on the special treatment and Self
and Physical Debility, Loss of Appetite, Pa
Indigestion, Spermatorrhœa, &c. Illustrated
showing the means by which the patient may
after Electricity and other FALSELY-CALLED re
Sent secure from observation, to any address
stamps.—Dr. SMITH, 8, Burton-crescent, Lond

THE SECRETS OF NATURE
PLAINED, &c., Forty Stamps. St
thirty eight stamps; Cartes-de-Visite, twenty
scarce works, two stamps.—M. STANLEY, 6
Rotherham.

JUST OUT.—A Novel and a Be
French Prints, richly coloured. Twe
stamps; twenty-four, all different, for t
ANDERSON, 32, Bidborough-street, London

READ THE "SECRET FRIE
Medical Guide for the cure of Nervou
Physical Debility, Lassitude, and all other ca
fidential and secret advice, arising from inju
This valuable work will be sent on receipt
Address, DR. J. A. BARNES, 30, Thornhill-cres

DR. HUNTER'S Special Lectures
on Health, its Restoration, and Happy I
marry, with advice to those who contemplate
out certain impediments which render marrie
directions for their speedy removal. Should
value health, strength, and manhood, and wis

30 Electromagnetic Telegraphone

Copper, iron, transfer gossip
Wapping, 1876

THE EXACT EVENTS surrounding Alexander Graham Bell's 1876 invention of the telephone have long been disputed. However, it is the view of the National Museum of the History of Sport, Orkney, that the definitive account is to be found in a contemporaneous news report by one John Wesley Ratt.

Ratt was a lover of all ball games and of drink and tittle-tattle. He later became the first association football and topless tribeswomen correspondent of the *News of the World*. He took a keen interest in the work and private life of Bell, and within a few minutes of the telephone's invention Ratt had managed to hack the device and listen to Bell's messages. A March 1876 feature by Ratt revealed:

RING! RING! Alexander Graham Bell today sensationally completed the design of his incredible telephone machine. Onlookers were left GASPING as boffin Bell turned on the contraption and it began to make NOISES.

And to the delight of the ecstatic egghead, the first recorded words that came out of the device were related to FOOTBALL. As the machine crackled into LIFE it was heard to say 'This is the Clubcall line of the Wanderers football club – stay on the line for news of a big-money transfer. Calls cost one guinea per minute and you must have the permission of the bill payer or a beadle to listen.'

Although there is no record of Wanderers recruiting or signing any player around that time, Ratt's faith in Bell and his telephone as a source of news remained undimmed. Had it not been for an unfortunate incident involving a payment to one of the Baker Street Irregulars for information about a glamorous lady jewel-thief posing as a Royal Engineers forward – a crime that saw Ratt hanged – this mutually profitable synergy of technology, sport and morally questionable news-gathering might have continued indefinitely.

PRICE ONE SHILLING.

BEING AN EXPOSITION OF THE MANY & MANIFEST
BENEFITS OF BARTHOLOMEW BOTWRIGHT'S NOVEL

AERIAL ARBITRATION ENGINE

OTHERWISE KNOWN TO ALL AS

THE HAWK-EYE

A PROVEN MECHANISM FOR THE SWIFT RESOLUTION
OF OTHERWISE VEXATIOUS & TROUBLING UMPIRING
DECISIONS IN REGARD OF LIMB BEFORE WICKET

(Artist's Impression)

YOUR LOCAL AGENT

Hamish Rupert & Sons

HAWKERS & SPORTING W'SALERS
LAMLASH, ISLE OF ARRAN

FROM THE MAKERS OF BARTHOLOMEW'S BOXES
— FINEST CRICKETING CODPIECES —
"ASK FOR NO OTHER WHEN YOUR MIDDLE STUMP IS AT STAKE"

31 Sports Technology Brochure

Printed ephemera
Isle of Arran, 1877

THIS CATALOGUE from a Victorian sporting goods company holds personal significance for me as the outfitters mentioned was established by my great-great-grandfather Hamish Rupert. That said, it is also, I believe, a major historical treasure.

Hamish made a not inconsiderable fortune in sporting goods in the mid-Victorian period. It is not now well known that many wealthy Scots were keen on cricket, seeing it as a means of social advancement in the Empire, and Hamish amassed quite a sum by selling cricket equipment to some of the oldest families north of the border. By the 1860s, due to playing on uneven, uncovered pitches with only sporrans for protection, birth-rates among the Scots cricket-playing classes had started to dip alarmingly as a result of injuries to the groin. Thus, when Hamish became the first man to import abdominal protectors into Scotland, he made a great deal of money. 'Rupert's Chuckie Stanes Defenders – Keep Ya Baws In Oor Box' became one of the best-known marketing lines of the decade, and Hamish one of the richest tradesmen on Prince's Street.

Buoyed by the success, Hamish poured vast resources into an attempt to corner the market in cricketing technology, working with a gifted, although deranged, English inventor named Bartholomew Botwright in the development of an LBW arbitration engine.

This brochure is a cruel snapshot of Hamish's success just before his terrible fall. During an 1877 visit to the Scots capital, Queen Victoria and her consort, Albert, attended a cricket match at The Grange where the Hawk-Eye was demonstrated to Her Majesty. Sadly, the device malfunctioned dreadfully, the bird of prey in question getting loose from its mooring on the popping crease and dealing Prince Albert a brutal nip to the royal unmentionables. Hamish compounded an already impossible situation by attempting to sell the stricken Prince an abdominal protector, and the ensuing scandal saw him black-balled from Edinburgh merchant society.

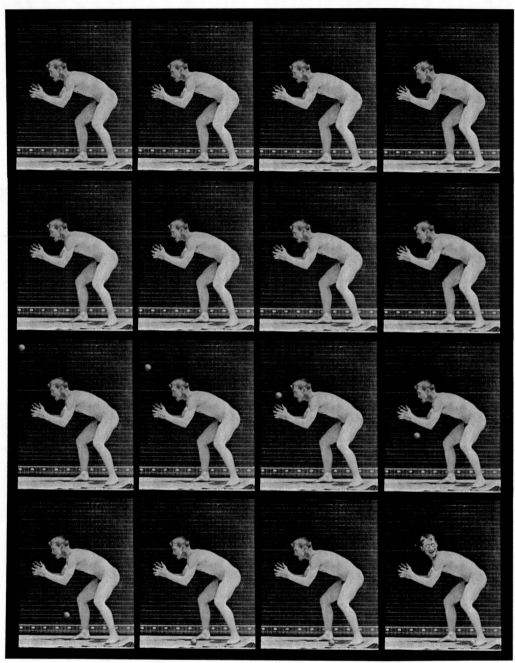

Copyright, 1878, by MUYBRIDGE.   ATYEO's Gallery, 417 Montgomery St., San Francisco.

THE CLUB CRICKETER IN MOTION.

Illustrated by

MUYBRIDGE

32 Biomechanical Study

Electro-photographic plate
Kingston-upon-Thames, 1878

THE PHOTOGRAPHIC PIONEER Eadweard Muybridge became
celebrated for his studies of horses galloping, as well as important
examinations in human movement such as throwing the discus,
wrestling, Scottish reeling, servant-thrashing and a very large and
important body of work featuring buxom young women jumping
up and down with no clothes on.

However, like all great innovators from Archimedes to Gary
Neville, Muybridge had many complex problems to solve in his
early exertions. The best camera he was able to construct in the
early 1870s could not capture motion at high speeds without
unacceptable blurring. Nor was he able to find any buxom young
women in Surrey willing to jump up and down with no clothes on.

Instead, he contented himself with observing and cataloguing the
kinetic action that he saw around him. An ardent follower of club
cricket, he took this series of photographs of a local club at play. He
was assisted, as always, by his comely Greek assistant, model and
muse, Zoopraxographica, after whom he named his method.

Fortunately, for the sake of the new art of photography and
Muybridge's commercial prospects, technology soon improved
to the point where he could take pictures of more exciting, and
competent, athletic endeavours. A move to more permissive
America also provided better opportunities for taking pictures of
naked women.

Left: It is thought that the fielder pictured opposite played for a gentleman's itinerant XI
called the Twenty Minuters. He was by no means the worst player on display for what
Wisden called 'the most wretched cricket team in the South of England, and probably the
entire civilised world.'

old etonians

Pater Familias
Most Advisory

TOFF JAM

Radiosendung ohne Genehmigung verboten

78 R

"We Are All
Presently Bound
for Wembley"

Binkley–Binkley

PLATTEROSCOPE

33⅓ The First FA Cup Recording

Gramophone disc
Royal Berkshire, 1882

THE 1882 FA CUP FINAL, contested by Old Etonians and Blackburn Rovers, was an eagerly anticipated affair, although police were concerned about crowd trouble involving Old Etonian Ultras, the famous public school having been plagued by a hooligan element among its support for some years. Defeat in the previous year's FA Cup Final at the hands of Old Carthusians had seen packs of drunken Old Etonians supporters roaming the streets around the Kennington Oval, committing random acts of bad behaviour including looting, littering and leaving the bottom buttons of their waistcoats done up.

Into this febrile atmosphere, the players of Old Etonians released the first FA Cup Final song. It was a grossly provocative composition, with lyrics penned by wing-half Binky 'Blinky' Binkley-Binkley, third Earl of Rottingdean, calculated to inflame and insult not just the Blackburn Rovers XI but polite society as a whole.

Verses such as: 'You'll never make it to the railway station/ Because we have engaged the services of all the Hansom Cabs in the vicinity'; 'My old man said be a Blackburn fan/I said steady on pater we no longer own any factories in that region of Great Britain' and 'Does your husband and 43 children know you are here?' were deemed so offensive that the record was banned.

Left: Disc from the personal collection of sporting musicologist John Barnes, Visiting Fellow of Cup Final Singles at RCA University, California.

34–35 Whiff-Waff Paddles

Stretched pumpkin skin and leather
London, 1894

MAYOR OF LONDON Boris Johnson was quite correct to assert that table tennis was a British sporting invention first played on the dining tables of the well-to-do. However, with typical modesty, Mr Johnson neglected to mention that one of his own family members was directly responsible for the genesis of the game.

At a London dinner held in 1894 to discuss logistics for a possible Olympic Games two years later, Reginald Patroclus Weimaraner Johnson, Olympic supremo, Nincompoop of the Garter and great-great-uncle of Boris, hosted Baron de Coubertin and sundry other French dignitaries. Coubertin made an off-hand remark about the quality of the *sauce béarnaise* that Johnson took in poor humour. Johnson wrote in his diary:

'I said "well then, sir, you blighter, sir," and I charged off to the kitchen. After an interlude when I had become briefly trapped in the hall cupboard, I eventually found the kitchen and I grabbed a saucepan to show the uppity Frenchie how we do a *béarnaise*. I ran back to the dining room but the thing was so dashed hot I could hardly hold onto it. I yelled out, "napkin!" but my idiotic butler, Coe, who is as deaf as a post and about as mobile, instead hurled a small pumpkin in my general direction. I swung the saucier at the gourd-like squash in my pain and fury, catching it right out of the middle of the pan and propelling it directly into the mush of poor old Coubertin.

'There was complete silence, save the doleful, slithering noise of the pumpkin's flesh as it dripped down his bib and tucker and onto the table with a sort of "whiff-waff" sound, and I knew right away that I was onto something rather splendid. I was jolly pleased with the invention of this new bat-and-ball pastime, but the Baron himself failed to see the good in it. No sense of humour, these foreigners.'

Her Ladyship's Intimate Exercises

#		
1	Wiggle your Woggle	One-step
2	The Tip Top Tuppence Tap !	Peabody Waltz
3	Shake that Booty (it's from the Maharajah's Palace)	Gay Gordon
4	The Drunken Sailor is now Abstained but still very much one of the Crew	Fo' Reel
5	Swinging is such Fun !	
6	Saturday Night Fever, Sunday Morning Quinine	Double Shag
7	One has Ninety-nine problems, but a brazen hussy is not among them	Secret Fling
		Foxytrot

DEPOSE

SWITZERLAND

WALTER MARTY HERITAGE

MY LADY'S BOX

36 Home Musical Exerciser

Wood, Lycra
Muswell Hill, 1899

THE END OF THE 19TH CENTURY saw a new affluent class of Briton move away from demanding manual labour (farming, fighting the French, bottling homebrewed bitumen) into more sedentary occupations like sighing at their housemaids, money laundering and being crippled with a nagging yet indefinable sense of something being not quite right.

Concomitantly, technological advances in transport and household appliances saw the bourgeoisie burning far fewer calories in their daily life, with vigorous sexual deviancy soon becoming the de facto number-one means of aerobic exercise for the middle class. This newly wealthy, fat and often uncomfortably sore tranche of society was extremely preoccupied with diets and personal fitness, and it was into this market that the 1899 My Lady's Box Home Musical Exerciser was launched.

The contraption played a repertoire of up-tempo popular songs and came with a printed handbook of instructions for exercises that a well-to-do lady could perform in the privacy and comfort of her own drawing room. The new keep-fit craze made celebrities of several popular gymnastic instructors, the most successful of them Mister (later Earl) Motivator. His enthusiastic exhortations ('Let's see those posteriors agitate rapidly, ladies and duchesses') could be read aloud by a servant while the woman of the house exercised in time to the music. The device sold in large numbers, but fell out of fashion when modernity's drive for efficiency and increased leisure time saw many prosperous women simply get their lady's maids to do the exercises for them.

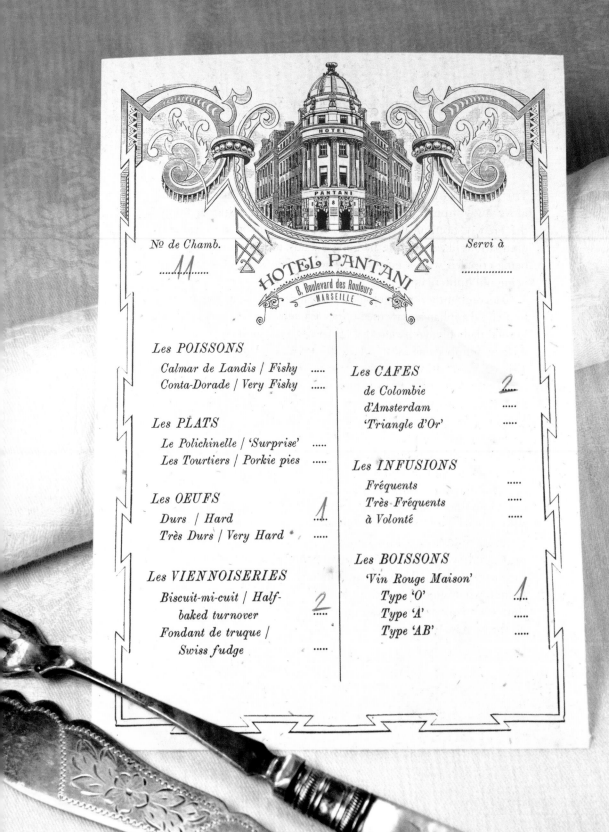

N° de Chamb.   Servi à

...11...   ....

HOTEL PANTANI
8, Boulevard des Rouleurs
MARSEILLE

Les POISSONS
Calmar de Landis / Fishy ......
Conta-Dorade / Very Fishy ......

Les PLATS
Le Polichinelle / 'Surprise' ......
Les Tourtiers / Porkie pies ......

Les OEUFS
Durs / Hard ...1...
Très Durs / Very Hard ......

Les VIENNOISERIES
Biscuit-mi-cuit / Half-
baked turnover ...2...
Fondant de truque /
Swiss fudge ......

Les CAFES
de Colombie ...2...
d'Amsterdam ......
'Triangle d'Or' ......

Les INFUSIONS
Fréquents ......
Très Fréquents ......
à Volonté ......

Les BOISSONS
'Vin Rouge Maison'
Type 'O' ...1...
Type 'A' ......
Type 'AB' ......

37 Breakfast Menu

Letterpress on bristol board, traces of unknown powder
Marseille, July 1903

THE FIRST TOUR DE FRANCE set the pattern for the sport's future, with some unconventional approaches to refuelling quickly becoming the norm. After a punishing second stage starting in Lyon, the exhausted riders arrived in Marseille, with the whole peloton staying overnight in the Hotel Pantani.

The proprietor of the hotel laid on everything and anything that the weary competitors could require. A guest only had to ask the night porter for '*un traversin supplémentaire*' (an 'extra bolster') and he would receive pints of blood, needles and (for a small additional fee) an iron bar with which to smash up his rival's bike, or indeed his rival.

Business boomed at the Hotel Pantani, which became a fixture on the cycling circuit, despite a guest fatality rate that *Le Guide Michelin* rated as 'unacceptably high for a three-star establishment'. The legendary cocktail, the Patani with a Twist (Cointreau, steroids, painkillers, angostura bitters and a dash of lime, served on the rocks or in a Spanish clinic), also takes its name from the hotel, although the barman credited with its invention later denied ever having worked there.

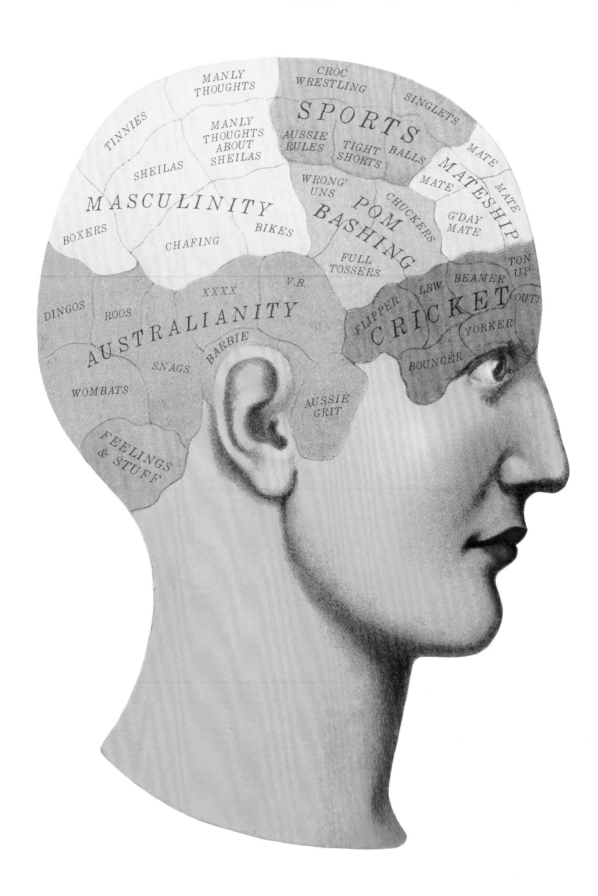

38 Mental Disintegration Mind Map

Pseudomedical diagram
Vienna, 1907

A COLLEAGUE AND RIVAL of Freud in Vienna, the pioneering sports psychologist Dr Stefan Väugh broke away from the Austrian School to work with a loose collation of like-minded analysts who formed what came to be known as the Australo-Austrian School and its more radical offshoot, the Australo-Austrian School of Hard Knocks.

It was the contention of Dr Väugh that the brain of the sportsman (*left*) was anatomically distinct from that of the ordinary person. His theories centred on the relationship between id, ego, super ego and team, and his work in the field of mental disintegration was as influential as it was ethically questionable. These typical extracts from his journals show an uncompromising attitude to therapy.

BOXING DAY, 1906
A young man came to see me today speculating that he had deep-seated issues involving childhood trauma. I told him to buck his bloody ideas up.

MARCH 12, 1907
Woman patient today complaining about nervousness and a sense of dread. I don't reckon she likes it up her, stick a short leg in and let her sniff the leather a bit.

JUNE 18, 1907
A new English patient. We explored some issues via free association. He crumbled like a dried dingo under the merest hint of a sledge. Pooftah?

Sadly, once psychotherapy gained recognition as a legitimate profession, Dr Väugh was promptly struck off for his controversial methods. He concentrated instead on publishing. His major works included *Slip Fielding and the Unconscious Mind*, *Beyond the Pleasure Principle: Taking One for the Baggy Green*, and three essays on the *Theory of Sexuality with Especial Reference to Pommie Batsmen*.

Eye of the Tiger-skin Rug

39 Entrance Music for a Fighter

Musical score
Canning Town, 1911

ONE OF THE MOST famous boxers of the pre-War period was
Montgomery Ffish-Tucker, a welterweight from a very good family
who divided his time between bare-knuckle boxing and big-game
hunting. He was among the first fighters to adopt a signature
'entrance' to the ring, emerging in a Japanese-style Kimono (made
from the pelt of a tiger he had knocked out with one left hook) to
the strains of the tune opposite, which was performed by a string
quartet. It made an intimidating, unusual sight and surely won
Ffish-Tucker many a bout before the first bell had even rung.

Ffish-Tucker had begun to box while up at Oxford and had been
the unofficial 'White Collar Boxing' Welterweight Champion, later
unifying that title with that of its more aristocratic cousin, 'Wing
Collar Boxing'. His high-water mark as a fighter came in 1911 when
he challenged for the British title against Reg 'The Executioner'
Ralston, so named due to his day-job as a hangman. Sadly, Ffish-
Tucker was not at his best. He had recently returned from a long
hunting expedition in Borneo where he had gone 15 rounds with
a rhinoceros and he was still carrying the effects of a horn to the
floating ribs. Ralston knocked him down twice in the first round
and, once he began attempting to noose Ffish-Tucker with the
ring's perimeter ropes, the referee stopped the contest.

Sensibly deciding to retire after that, Ffish-Tucker began to work
as a promoter, organising the fights of a Prince Naseem, billed as 'The
Persian Sensation'. On Ffish-Tucker's suggestion, Prince Naseem
would also enter the ring to the tune of 'Eye of the Tiger-skin Rug',
festooned in lavish jewellery including a brooch made from the eye
of a magnificent striped Bengal that Ffish-Tucker had defeated, not
under Queensberry rules, in an unlicensed back-street contest in
Mombasa. Both fighter and impresario made considerable fortunes
but saw their stars wane when the WWF (World Wildlife Fund)
captured the public imagination.

40–48 Commemorative Stamps

Perforated paper squares, gum
Mount Pleasant, 1912

IN HONOUR OF British medallists at the 1912 London Olympics, the Royal Mail produced this set of 'A Splendid Effort' stamps. There was considerable debate over which of the Olympic heroes and heroines merited recognition in the collection. The decisions not to commemorate the achievements of Lucien Lightshow-Carter, who took bronze in men's Greco-Roman cocktail shaking, and His Grace the Bishop of Lincoln, who won gold in mixed cavorting, were particularly controversial.

In protest, some of the clergy in Lincolnshire took to painting post-boxes in their parishes black to express their disgust at the snub of the popular prelate. His Grace was the sort of muscular Christian whose hearty enthusiasm for sports of all kinds – he took a Blue for hare coursing at Oxford, and four times represented Bishops against Cardinals in the notoriously violent annual football match in Vatican City – made him a popular, manly and well-liked figure across all strata of society.

However, recently discovered letters from the London Olympic Committee to the Royal Mail reveal that there was a suspicion the Bishop's gold was tainted. Nothing was ever proved, but the strong suggestion is that his Grace had been using performance-enhancing drugs (probably incense, possibly over-strength communion wine) in both training and competition. It was felt that to draw too much attention to his feats might attract the scrutiny of the Olympic movement's drug-testing unit, who were clamping down hard on banned substances and especially on competitors – his Grace among them – who sought to gain an unfair advantage by refusing to smoke tobacco.

49 Promotional Postcard

Sensationalist photographs on paper
Plymouth, 1913

During the late-19th century, diving was a popular pastime in Britain, and celebrated *plongeurs* such as Tinker 'Tanker' Tonker, the Salko Sisters and Dominic, Earl of Pinner were as famous and fêted as footballers today. However, the industrial revolution and the resulting pollution had made diving into rivers and lakes extremely hazardous in certain parts of the country.

While perfecting his double-somersault-with-butler in an east London reservoir, the British diving poster boy Master Thos. Daley nearly lost a foot, so acidic was the water. Thenceforth, he would dive only in this suit, which was considered daringly revealing when worn in mixed company and caused dozens of impressionable young women to swoon.

50 War Poetry

Indian ink on poppy paper
Belgium, 1914

The sweat, the foul stench, the mud. Always the mud. The senseless, sense-shattering thudding of the long-range attacks. The stretchers. The defenders, ever weary, driven on by their heartless commander. The remorseless toll on the young bodies. The deathly, hollow cry of 'attack!' And always the mud.

THIS MOVING PASSAGE comes from the diary of the little-known First World War poet Archibald Bathgate (1893–1915) and describes his experiences playing for the Bolton Wanderers team managed by Samuel 'Big Sam' Pilkington in a Cup match away at Bradford Linkin Park Avenue in 1913. The savage tactics popularised by Big Sam were to set Association Football in the North back by many years; indeed, so brutal were his training methods that whole regiments were formed of men eager to get to the Front just to be excused his pre-season sessions.

Bathgate was a third-generation wool miner, a specialised local industry where workers were sent down a pit with a heavy loom strapped to their backs. During the 55 or so years that wool mining was practised in the Bolton region, no wool was ever found underground. However, it did breed a generation of very small, stocky men with a low-centre of gravity: ideal wing-half cannon fodder for Big Sam's teams.

Called up to the First XI by Big Sam in 1914, Bathgate acted swiftly and was among the first in his village to join up for the Army. He was at the first battle of Ypres in 1914 and found it 'appallingly horrible, like a Hell come to Earth. But not as bad as watching Big Sam eat a breakfast bap with his mouth open while he made you practise defending a free-kick.' Bathgate was on the front line for the famous Christmas Day Truce of 1914, writing about it in what would become his collection *War: What Is It Good For?* He was killed a year later by gas; Big Sam tried to have him court-marshalled for feigning injury.

Lottery

No kiddies playing, no plum pudding. No fire.
Just the icy rifle and a mean little fag.
A cry comes down the line. Heart thumps.
The Germans are out in No Man's Land.
Is this our Christmas Day? Our day of death?

But not today boys, not today,
Today we play at football, not at war.
Eleven of ours and eleven of theirs
Shivering young men. Are we so different?
The Germans will be well organised, Brian.

Two-One up with minutes left to play
Young Tommy charges down the wing.
Hits a shot with fearsome power —
It hits their full-back on the hand.
The ref waves play on, the bastard.

Of course they go and equalise.
Ends two-all. The agony of penalties,
Brave old Sergeant Bill steps up —
And puts it over the bar. The Germans win.
You can't practise them, can you?

At least he had the bottle to take one,

51 Fantastical Map

Dwarf art, Elvish words, Orcsford commas
Middle Earth, Third Age 2941 (Númenórean Calendar)

DURING HIS TIME at Pembroke College, Oxford, J.R.R. Tolkien was a keen rugby player. He was disappointed to miss some of the 1925 season with a concussion picked up either during a November game against St Edmund Hall or during a vigorous debagging celebration after that match.[1]

Confined to his digs and woozy, Tolkien worked on what would become *The Hobbit*; sketching and mapping the climactic clash of that story – the Battle of the Five Nations – and doing some initial work on the correct Elvish pronunciations of the names of the pets of some of the distant relatives of some of the minor characters who may or may not have met the heroes of his story.

Sadly, these abandoned sketches were not published during Tolkien's lifetime, but they will be released in a major motion picture franchise of seven films entitled *The Twin Posts: Lord of the Rugby*. Sir Ian McKellen will reprise his role as Gandalf, with Jonathan Davies as heroic hobbit Bilbo and Brian Moore taking over from Cate Blanchett as the ethereal elf queen Galadriel.

---

1   Tolkien's diary from the day after the match said: 'Much enjoyable carousing last night but today I feel like the Great Orc Teague, son of Chilcott son of Uttley, Dark Lord of Nausea and Bane of the merrie folk of Al Kazeltser, has been using my head to perform his brutal ablutions.' This suggests either that the author had been well refreshed the night before, or suffered a serious head trauma, or had perhaps attempted to read *The Silmarillion: Chronicles of the Laws Governing the Use of Hands in the Ruck* without recourse to strong analgesics.

52 Military Intelligence Report

Semi-invisible ink on flash paper
Classified location just outside Dieppe, 1940

IN THE PERIOD leading up to Britain's active involvement in the Second World War, reconnaissance of the French Maginot Line was a top priority. The success of that defensive system in keeping Hitler at bay would self-evidently be vital to Britain's own military situation, and Secretary of State for War, Leslie Hore-Belisha speculated that a fine cricketing mind might be well suited to analysing the tactical weaknesses of the line.

He wrote to Douglas Jardine to offer the post of Chief Maginot Assessor but received a two-word telegram in reply, only one word of which is printable ('____ trousers'). Casting his net wider, Hore-Belisha considered that the key Maginot issues of communication and positioning might be well examined by a football man. Thus, he tracked down a dour, astute Scots Engineer and football enthusiast from Clackmannanshire.

Major Alan Hansen's withering assessment of the French frailties proved all too accurate but he drew no pleasure from being proved right. He was often called upon during the War to assess a defensive structure or system, but eventually the top brass grew exasperated with his unfailing verdicts of 'terrible, just terrible'. Hansen was sidelined into a desk job, and disappeared altogether after the War, rumoured to be 'working for the Reds'.

FORTERESSE MODERNE
A FLANC DE COLLINE
TYPE «LIGNE MAGINOT

1940 - TOP SECRET

he French have got a serious problem here. The way
these turrets are positioned, you've got huge gaps
because they're defending the space zonally and th
always leads to problems believe you me,

The Germans are efficient, they're well organised, a
they've just come through the Ardennes Forest like the
nobody there, which there isn't because the French are all ou
of position. That leaves Sedan here totally isolated and the
Germans have swept through at pace, and there's one thing
any defensive commander will tell you is a nightmare,
and that's a Blitzkrieg tank attack at pace,

Marshal Philippe Pétain says that the

Do me a favour, Terrible, rea
terrible defendi
uphill b
Wednesda
shocking
with kids
absolutely

Hansen, A.

53 Advice for American Owners of Football Clubs in Britain

Small casebound book, 32 pages
War Office, 1942

WINSTON CHURCHILL was well aware of football's impact upon wartime morale, and invited wealthy Americans to inject much-needed capital into major clubs. The covert Foreign Owner Yanks Committee (FOYC) insisted that all would-be foreign owners pass stringent tests of their suitability for owning a club, featuring questions such as 'Have you got some money?' and 'Can we have some of your money?'

Despite this rigorous financial questionnaire, some Americans managed to take control of clubs via debt-heavy Lend-Lease schemes. In the case of Manchester United and P. Montgomery Roosterbender III Junior, the Massachusetts poultry and ice-hockey magnate was able to buy the club on a vague promise to send some chicken sandwiches over for the war effort, with the club misguidedly agreeing to a debt-purchase structure of such exorbitant interest rates that the Roosterbender family still owned a leg of Ryan Giggs as recently as 2011.

The FOYC, though, could hardly afford to be picky and was desperate to attract would-be American investors, producing this little pamphlet as part of a propaganda drive. A valuable snapshot of both Anglo–American wartime relations and British sporting life, it provides instruction on the rules of the sport, supporter culture, and how to extinguish a burning effigy with the minimum of fuss.

Right: On loan from the Glazer Collection at the Bodlean Library, an American Studies foundation that borrows books from the Bodlean Library.

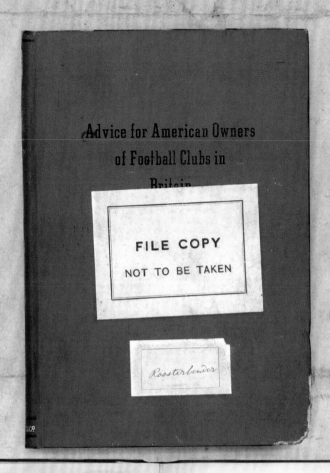

Advice for American Owners
of Football Clubs in
Britain

FILE COPY

NOT TO BE TAKEN

Roosterbender

ATTENDING A FOOTBALL (SOCCER) MATCH

Bear in mind that the game itself is rather boring and goals (scores) are rare. Consider enjoying the game from, for instance, Florida rather than attending in person.

If you do visit the stadium, notice that the British enjoy a good sing-song and set great store by affectionate teasing. Look out for chants like "Yanks out", "We want our club back" and "Go back to Boston you greedy bastards" at matches. These are traditional welcomes and are all examples of the famed British sense of humor.

Don't worry if you have been on the wrong side of the law back home. Fraud, corruption and bankruptcy are no barriers to being a fit and proper person to own a football club. Remember, you are doing our British allies a great favour by borrowing money from them to buy their soccer teams.

Many supporters, especially in the North East, are tired of the plain old names for their soccer stadiums and will enthusiastically welcome a change of name to, for instance, the Sherman Q. Gumboggle Powdered Meat Bowl.

One of the highlights of the British calendar is Guy Fawkes Night on November 5th, where a 'Guy' or effigy is burned in the streets. So popular has this become, it is now common to welcome foreign visitors by making an effigy of them and burning it. This is not restricted to November.

54 Crown Beat Bowling Manuscript

Typescript on scorecards
Taunton, 1951

REPLETE WITH REFERENCES to drugs, sex and unsuitable footwear, Jack Kerouac's *On the Road* famously caused a literary and moralistic storm when it was published in 1951. However, less well known is the fact that Kerouac was most influenced not by his muse Neal Cassady, nor be-bop, nor even 'tea', but by the Somerset Crown Green Bowling and Beat Poetry scene.

Pre-eminent of these radical young bowlers was David Bryant, known best in later life for smoking a pipe and always being on the television on Saturday afternoon winning bowls tournaments. As a younger man, before bowls seduced him completely, it was the life of the road and free-form prose that most captured the imagination of this restless soul. He would take long drives across Somerset, barely stopping to rest, driving at great speeds from his home in Clevedon sometimes as far as Midsomer Norton in the east of the county. His constant companion on these trips was the renegade bowler and visionary George Twelvetrees: a brilliant, if erratic, presence around the crown green and a lover of intoxicants from cider to Westcombe Cheddar (extra mature).

Inspired by Twelvetrees' lust for life and their poetic, frenetic conversations on the way to bowls matches, Bryant would chronicle their adventures in furious typing sessions around the back of the bowling pavilion. He did not wish to break his flow by changing sheets of paper in his typewriter, so he would glue bowls scorecards together to make a continuous roll. Kerouac most probably visited Somerset, possibly Ilfracombe, and took both Bryant's methods and style back to New York.

never liked Ginsberg not as a poet or a bowler
and I told him as much that if he came down to
Somerset then we could sort it out for once and
for all but then he went missing in New Orleans
for months and I took to living out in Frome. I was
going to go all the way out into the west and
maybe get a little cabin in Montana or Minehead
and a girl and just work on my backhand and chop
wood and eat soup and just be but in the end
there was the North Devon invitational and I
didn't make the journey.

George was driving and the little Morris Minor
was speeding and hurtling and charging around
those bends like Charlie Parker blowing in the
hot night or like Clevedon mixed pairs winning
the County Plate at Wookey Hole when I got up off
the carpet to take the last end back in September
when we were nowhere.

George always drove like he bowled, wild and
glorious and free but with no attention to blind
spots on his backhand side. It was like the road
was a drainpipe on a slope and he was a bowl just
hurtling down it to the inevitable and he never
even considered that it could deviate to the
forehand or the backhand or any hand just
straight, straight and fast and mad. We were so
close to the side of the road, almost in the
hedge, that I could see individual twigs and
berries and in one of them a blackbird that I
looked right in the eye and with its yellow beak
like a shard of the sun. George was laughing and
laughing with the whole mad joyous wild freedom
of it all and I look over at the dashboard and we
are going 20 25 30 miles per hour and he's got
this big grin all over his face and he is
shouting "David boy we are going to bowl some
tonight".

I am gripping the passenger door and thinking
will this ride ever stop and then I start to lose
myself and travel not in the car or with it but as
it. I am the car. The car is me. It is all car. I am
in the car but I'm not in it and I am hurtling and
speeding into the great wide open space of the
gutter like a forehand draw gone wild and I am a
jack, a bowl, a target and the green and my pipe
all in one at once. The road is the guard bowl
guarding the jack and I am coming down the green
and bang I am going to knock that jack out of the
way and into the starry heaven of the gutter and
it will be my end and their end and the end of
everything. And I laugh and laugh as the Morris
crosses the A37 at Chewton Mendip and we stop for
some cider.

55 The Superb Owl

Preserved bird
Los Angeles, 1957

THIS MAJESTIC STUFFED Chegwin's Owl, a critically endangered bird of prey native to the Rockies, was, for a brief time, the most revered prize in American sport. In 1957, as the champions of the rival American Football conferences prepared to meet in a final, a telegram was sent from the National League commissioner, Patrick Fitzwilliam, to his American League counterpart, William Fitzpatrick. He suggested a contest for the 'Super Bowl' and that, as a bit of sport, the conference which produced a trophy first would have the honour of providing the prize.

In his haste to get one over on Fitzwilliam, Fitzpatrick failed to read the message properly. He grabbed his rifle, broke into the nearby Binghamton Bird Sanctuary and shot this Chegwin's Owl in the body, head and beak. It is a tribute to the taxidermist's skill that he was able to get the lead-filled carcass into any condition at all, and it was proudly paraded by American League dignitaries before the match, Fitzpatrick crowing, 'How d'ya like that Superb Owl?'

The blunder was apparent right away and, to hoots of derision, Fitzpatrick dashed out of the stadium in embarrassed panic. He managed to buy a trophy at a nearby shoe repairers but there was no time to engrave it, so the victorious Green Bay Packers were presented with a small shield honouring 'Mom of the Year'. They launched a lawsuit against Fitzpatrick, as did the family of the owl.

Fitzpatrick fled to rural Mexico where, in a cruel twist of fate, he was killed by a condor. Unfortunately, the local undertaker died the same day and, in the fierce heat, the only way to preserve Fitzpatrick's body for shipping back to Binghamton was to have him stuffed. Even this solution proved problematic. With the village taxidermist having gone missing, Fitzpatrick's corpse was prepared for burial by the man next-best suited for the task: the local burrito vendor. The family back in America refused to take delivery of their beloved relative, because guacamole was leaking out of him, and sent the body back to Mexico. In the end, the late gridiron pioneer suffered the indignity of being mounted on the wall of Chico's Tacos.

56 SLAAM!

Oils and egg tempura on canvas, 1963

ANDREW MURRAY had been a talented but frustrated and overlooked Scottish painter[1] for nearly a decade – until one vibrant exhibition in New York changed everything.

Initially dismissed as little more than a copyist of Henman and the Wimbledon School of abstract petulism (early Murray works included the immature *Because Mother Said To Do It* and the startling but ultimately insubstantial *My Legs Hurt: Tantrum 6-4 6-4 6-0*), Murray was radicalised by a meeting with the Czech brutalist I. Lendl. Becoming a pupil of the pioneering expressionlessist,

Murray began to neglect his previous method of internalised self-loathing in favour of a more measured, confident approach engendered by a new-found mastery of big-pointillist techniques and a move away from apologetic semifinalism.

Under the sway of his Svengali-like master, he produced a series of brilliant works, beginning with *Ivan Is My Mummy Now*, then *Judy Who?* and this, the defiant masterpiece that made him the darling of the New York scene: *Slaam!*

---

[1] Murray loathed being grouped with English artists, dismissing them 'a bunch of Sassenach snobs with their Hay Wains and World Cup qualifications'.

57 Encrypted Microdot

Miniature file storage device
Sydney, 1964

THE PRESS MAY have mocked Australian cricket for its preparation of 'secret dossiers' on opponents, but no respectable voice in the sports history community was raised against Cricket Australia's methods, even when its reports were pushed under the wrong doors.

Indeed, the country has a rich espionage tradition. In the 1960s, Australia wished to move out of Britain's shadow and assert herself on the world stage. The creation of the Australian Secret Service (known by its initials or its official agency title M8) saw the country proudly play its role in the Cold War.[1]

As with much in Australian life, the M8 section regarded sporting excellence as *the* yardstick of trustworthiness, and recruited players from the country's major sports. Sadly, the 1961 capture of a cell of Australian Rules Footballers in Moscow – their cover blown as they drew attention to themselves by wearing only vests outside during the harsh Russian winter – proved a diplomatic embarrassment. M8 thereafter relied on cricketers for its intelligence gathering.

The object opposite is an original Microdot from 1964, smuggled back to Australia in a tin of Victoria Bitter. To throw counter-espionage agents off the scent, an M8 operative would drink 50 cans of beer on the flight home, and then urinate out the dot. The discomfort in passing the sensitive information was numbed by the alcohol, and it was of course impossible for the KGB to search every can of beer belonging to every Australian traveller.

This microdot, whose contents were recently declassified, contains information from an agent, codename Alfie. He was dispatched to spy on a suspected high-ranking KGB operative who was posing as a chef at the Soviet Embassy. Alfie reported: 'Russian bloke, 50s, fat. Not played cricket before. Vulnerable to 90 mph short ball? Also try Brezhnev out with yorker early on? Eyebrows make him look like a pussy. Suspect against short-pitched quick bowling or having nuclear bomb dropped on him?'

---

[1] The activities of the M8 section in the 1960s formed the basis of a series of popular spy thrillers by the Australian author Pongo Lecarry, the best-known being *The Man who came in from the Dunny*, *Tinker Taylor Pommie Pooftah* and *That Ruskie looks like a Sheila*.

58–61 Pop Art Prints

Limited-edition seriagraphs
New York, 1965

The first Duckworth-Lewis table only sold 10,000 copies but everyone who bought it became a first-class umpire.

THIS QUOTE, variously attributed to Brian Eno and Dickie Bird, sums up the colossal cricketing impact of the 1965 meeting of two remarkable men: Duckworth and Lewis.

Duckworth had already achieved legendary status in the New York mathematics scene, and the 'Mathappenings' at his 47th Street Prime Number Factory were a magnet for models, rock stars, socialites and cricket scorers. Strolling through Greenwich Village one evening, Duckworth spotted a bespectacled young man deeply engrossed in a Sudoku puzzle, and approached him. It was, of course, Lewis: young, troubled, relentlessly ambitious and brilliant at sums. The connection was instantaneous and era-defining.

Duckworth and Lewis began work on a project that would combine their major obsessions: the relationship between consumerism and the creative process; the notion of fame as a work of art; and mitigating the unfortunate effect of rain on limited-overs cricket matches. Work at Duckworth's Exploding the Precipitation Inevitable studio eventually resulted in the seminal The Duckworth-Lewis and Nico Method's *Table of Runs Required Versus Overs Left.*

Sadly, argument about how the Method might behave under 20-over conditions caused an irreparable rift. The partnership was abruptly severed, but the influence on cricketing statisticians would be immeasurable. As Duckworth famously said: 'In the future everyone will be famous for 15 overs (DL method)'.

THAT IS DEFINITELY A GOAL COMRADE

62 Eye chart

Letters of varying size on card
Wembley, 1966

THIS EYE TEST was given to all prospective referees and linesmen prior to the 1966 World Cup. It was administered by a Wembley opticians that, according to the West German press, was owned by senior figures in the FA hierarchy and which only issued a 'pass' mark to certain carefully selected candidates.

A Football Association inquiry found that Ramsey & Sons Eye Care had no case to answer.

63 Traction Man

Moulded plastic, medical gauze and string
Tottingham, 1967

As GEORGE BEST became football's first superstar and marketeers awoke to the possibilities offered by glamorous soccer players, a new toy captured the imagination of British youth. The first range of footballer figurines was popular among little boys, but a brainwave by the manufacturer Pallistertoy opened up the market to both boys and girls.

In 1967, they released the Anderton Traction Man, a permanently injured footballer toy. Boys liked to imagine the football heroics the Anderton might perform if he could regain fitness for more than a day or two at a time, while little girls loved treating and nursing the permanently crocked doll. The Anderton Traction Man was an enormous success with children of both genders, and started a entire range of dolls with gripping hands, easily dislocated knees and real-feel brittle bones, perhaps the most famous of which was the Talking Doctor model.

On pulling the cord of the Talking Doc, the figure would deliver realistic sports injury phrases such as 'We're all on our way to physiotherapy', 'Come on you outpatients' and 'When the Spurs come hobbling in'. Sadly, the toys invariably broke under the slightest touch and, when the 1970s saw the arrival of a range of Leeds United Bully Trolls, Traction Man and his friends were relegated to the status of a historical curiosity.

¡HOLY FRIJOLES!
Especial Mexico
Jumpy Bean
In the Sauce
90% Natural
Very Tasting
The Frijoles with Cojones!*
*minimum 15% cojones

64 Mexican Jumping Beans

Tinned pulses in brine
Mexico City, 1968

ON OCTOBER 18th 1968, Bob Beamon leapt into sporting immortality with a long jump of 8.90 metres. He set a record that stood for a remarkable 23 years, but Beamon himself never again jumped more than 8.22 metres. It was previously believed that a 'perfect storm' of altitudinal and climatic conditions aided Beamon in his astonishing feat, but sporting historians now believe that the American athlete may have had some dietary assistance.

On arriving in Mexico, Beamon had taken to eating Mexican jumping beans at every meal. He favoured the brand pictured opposite due to its very high protein content; laboratory analysis later revealed the contents to be unusually rich in unusual animal by-products, high-twitch muscle fibres, synthetic flammable fibres and rubber. Scientific studies found that side-effects of eating the beans could include serious flatulence, and it is possible that Beamon's famously wind-assisted jump may have been gastrointestinal rather than meteorological.

Returning to the USA, Beamon became the face of a new brand of baked beans – Bob Beansmons – but they were discontinued due to poor sales and poor life expectancy for customers. Beamon was never again able to recapture the precise alchemy of thin air and thick, sulphurous propulsion he enjoyed in Mexico '68. Nonetheless, his record stood until Tokyo 1991, when it was broken by Mike Powell with a mark of 8.95 metres, now thought to have been achieved with the assistance of a high-tech take-off board and a diet of 1,000-year-old pickled tofu.

65 Seminal Hard Rock Iconography

LP Sleeve artwork
Bron-Yr-Aur, 1971

A CHANCE SNOWDONIA MEETING between two great foursomes may have changed the course of sporting – and musical – history. In 1971, the rock band Led Zeppelin were staying at their Bron-Yr-Aur cottage; Welsh rugby legends Gerald Davies, Barry John, Gareth Edwards and J.P.R. Williams had gone on an extended pub crawl around Wales to celebrate their Five Nations Grand Slam triumph. The two groups met in the nearby Black Dog & Tackle pub and, after some initial hostility over which had the next go on the bar billiards table, struck up a conversation based on J.P.R. Williams and John Paul Jones approvingly comparing sideburns.

A drinking competition between Barry John and John Bonham continued long into the night back at the cottage as all eight decamped there. Music folklore suggests that an impromptu session led to a recording of *Down The Blind Side*, later reworked as *Black Mountain Side*, and that an early version of *No Quarter* may have been initially conceived as *Wing Three-quarter*. Sadly no master tapes survive, but Gerald Davies – an accomplished artist – did sketch these concepts for the cover design, including avatars of himself and his three team-mates, probably influencing Page when he came to produce *Led Zeppelin IV*.

For their part, the rock and roll legends also inspired the rugby greats. J.P.R. Williams reported that his notorious 50-yard run to punch a South African opponent in the 1974 Lions Tour was, in part, a tribute to the gloriously savage way John Bonham hit his snare drum; and that the famous '99 call' may have been inspired by Bonham doing something unprintable with a female fan and an ice-cream.

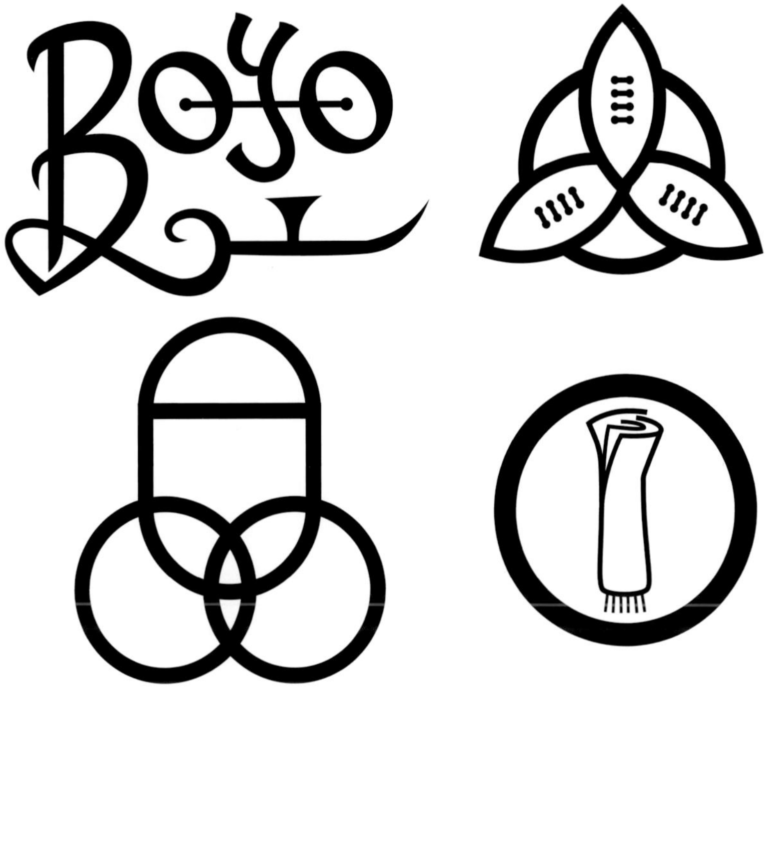

66–70 Russian Dolls

Wood, steroid-based paints
Belarus, 1972

PRODUCED BY THE Soviet Ministry of Children's Toys (Sporting and Nuclear Division) in the early Seventies, this set of dolls depicts the Testosterova sisters, the preeminent gymnastic dynasty of the era.

Born into poverty in Minsk to a circus ringmaster and a disgraced prima ballerina, the children were working as acrobats before they could walk, and in some cases after they stopped being able to walk. As the surviving ones grew, they were given a special training and 'dietary' programme by the notorious Central Circus School in Moscow, and in 1970 five of the sisters, all aged under ten, were sent on a demonstration tour of European capitals. Western observers were stunned by the discipline, strength and deep, booming voices of Valeriya, Elena, Oksana, Svetlana and Mo'Neeq, and marvelled at their feats of lifting, pyramid-building and moustache-growing. So accelerated was their physical development, in fact, that the eldest, Valeriya, began drawing a state pension by the age of 11.

The Testosterova sisters would surely have come away with a hatful of medals at the 1972 Olympics, but a dispute over which events to enter split the Sports Ministry. Some officials were convinced that the best chance lay in the women's team all-around gymnastics, but others were sure that a possible clean sweep of medals in the men's shot put and light-heavyweight boxing was the most sensible course of action. A bureaucratic deadlock could not be broken, and by the time the Montreal Olympics came around, the troupe had drifted out of top-level gymnastics to work variously on a building site, as a nightclub bouncer and, in the case of the second youngest, Svetlana, to play for Hull Kingston Rovers at the back of the scrum, becoming at eight years old the club's youngest overseas signing for more than a century.

Raakte de aardappel wafel!

Coaching handleiding 66.21.3 v2.1

71–72 Tactical Condiments

Full English and sauce bottles
Kilburn, 1974

IN THE 1970s, the legendary Dutch coach Rinus Michels visited England regularly, largely to refresh his memory of how football should not be played. Delayed by Jubilee Line engineering works on his way to Wembley one morning, he exited the underground at Kilburn and stopped at Rosie's Café for a meal that would, despite its unlikely and humble origins, have huge cultural significance. He wrote in his diary:

> The café was crowded but I asked to share a table which had three guys at it – I never like being forced to sit in one fixed table so it didn't cause a problems for me. One of them, a builder, was demonstrating to the others a goal he had scored in his Sunday League game, moving the pepper pots and sauce bottles around.
>
> As I was watching his rudimentary tactical explanation, I started to examine also his breakfast. It occurred to me that the traditional English breakfast was out-dated, rigid – the bacon down the side, the fried bread forming a wall, the beans kept disconnected away from the egg, the immobile tomato. Why should the fried-up have to be this way?
>
> I began to move items around on the man's plate – a piece of bacon here, overlapping with the fried slice, a mushroom here popping up, there receding into the egg yolk, a free-form dollop of brown sauce working in perfect harmony in alongside red sauce, a Withdrawn (or False) Sausage, all coming together in one glorious breakfast whole.
>
> The builder man was resistant to my revolutionising of his plate and told me if I did not stop rearranging his breakfast he would start rearranging my face. I told him this would not be necessary and left quietly, sure in the knowledge that the English are a generation at least behind my concept of Total Breakfast.

Left: This Total Breakfast model is used for tactical analysis at the Ajax All-day Academy and has kindly been loaned to the Museum.

73 Movie Script

Melodramatic dialogue on paper
Hollywood, 1980

IT WAS VARIOUSLY called 'the greatest story never told', dismissed as an unfilmable monstrosity and cited as the picture that would usher in a new 'Golden Age' of Hollywood. It featured some of the most compelling characters ever to bestride this sporting stage of ours, attracted the attention of the brightest stars on the planet and eventually collapsed under the sheer weight of ego, excess and decadence. I am referring, as any *cinéaste sportive* will know, to the never-released, notorious feature film about snooker in the first half of the 1980s, *Crucible of the Gods: Baize of Glory*.

The emergence of a class of brilliant, captivating, highly marketable young snooker stars such as Terry Griffiths, Dennis Taylor and Steve Davis proved an irresistible lure for Hollywood. A feeding frenzy began to find the right vehicle for these new alpha males of the snooker hall whose collective popularity was thought potentially to exceed even that of the Rat Pack. John Virgo, working in collaboration with a friend of his cousin's called Nerys, who owned a typewriter, produced a searing script about the passion, the rivalries, the outrageous lifestyles and the lavish waistcoats of the young Turks of the table.

Robert De Niro famously challenged Al Pacino to a fist fight for the right to play Alex Higgins. With Orson Welles as Ray Reardon and Clint Eastwood as the uncompromising Australian Eddie Charlton, production was to start in Los Angeles and Sheffield in the Summer of 1982. But it was the casting of Diane Keaton as Virgo's cousin's friend Nerys that derailed the film. Virgo had negotiated ultimate creative power of veto on the project by threatening to have Jim Davidson perform stand-up comedy in America, and refused point-blank to proceed unless Grace Kelly appeared in Keaton's place. When the Princess Consort of Monaco died in the September, the film, on Virgo's insistence, died with it.

INT. THE CRUCIBLE SNOOKER THEATRE - NIGHT

A single spotlighted snooker table. Some VERY HANDSOME RUGGED MEN
are practising trickshots such as potting a yellow into a wicker basket
in the right baulk pocket. The rain falls outside. ALEX HIGGINS enters.

                        ALEX HIGGINS
              To be sure, to be sure, it's raining out
              there so it is. One day a real rain's gonna
              come and wash all this scum off the streets.

                        STEVE DAVIS
              You and me Higgins. Let's go, now.

                        TERRY GRIFFITHS
              Leave it Steve, Boyo. He's got a weapon.

                        ALEX HIGGINS
              That's a snooker cue, begorrah. Oh Danny Boy.

                        TERRY GRIFFITHS
              Fair play, so it is.

                        EDDIE CHARLTON
              The question you have to ask yourself, Higgins,
              is "do you feel lucky?„ Well do ya, punk?" Can you
              get the two snookers required and still clean up,
              even with a red on the cushion like that, strewth?

Everyone turns as NERYS enters. She is a busty stunner.

                        NERYS
              If anyone can, John Virgo can.

JOHN VIRGO enters. His waistcoat speaks of a man totally comfortable in
himself, a man of substance. He has a beard you could lose yourself in.

                        JOHN VIRGO
              Alright Nerys love just let me chalk my cue.

NERYS blushes in a sexy way so to speak. JOHN VIRGO pots all the balls.
ALEX HIGGINS leaves, humiliated.

                        NERYS
              Oh John you were magnificent

                        JOHN VIRGO
              Just doing my job, little lady.

They kiss. EVERYONE cheers and practises snooker trickshots.

On the paper tape:
- too much Chicken Chow Mein
- slow midfield dynamo
- Number 118 with gravy
- A wise man always
- defend near post on Corners
- Get it up to the big man
- Confucius say...
- play two holdi...
- ...her special noodles
- ...y a fool
- ...midfielders

RONOTRON3 80

Keyboard key legends:

Top number row:
EDIT	AND	THEN	TO					GRAPHICS	RUBOUT
4	4	2	4	4	2	4	4	2	0

QWERTY row (above): PLOT · UNPLOT · SUB · RUN · RAN · RETURN · SWEET · SOUR · PORK · SPRINT
Keys: Q W E R T Y U I O P
QWERTY row (below): SIGN · CROSS · TAN · INT · RND · STR$ · CHRI$T · CODE · PEEK · JAB
Symbols on keys: "" OR STEP <= <> >= $ ( ) "

ASDF row (above): NEW · STOP · SAVE · SPRINT · DIM · BOOT · FAST · REBOOT · GOSUB · GOAL · CODE · LIST · WELLY IT
Keys: A S D F G H J K L FUNCTION NEW LINE UP
ASDF row (below): SPRING · ROLLS · SUM · SGN · ABS · SQR · VAL · LEN · USR
Symbols: SLOW ** − + =

ZXCV row (above): COPY · CLEAR · CONT · SCORE · ROLL · PRWN · CRACKR$ · BREAK
Keys: SHIFT IT Z X C V B N M . £ PACE
ZXCV row (below): LN · EXP · AT · IN KEY$ · NOT · π
Symbols: : ; ? / * < > ,

74 Supercomputer

Moulded plastic, silicon, fortune cookies
Manchester, 1981

THERE HAS BEEN no greater friend to the Museum than the legendary manager, linguist and victim-of-political-correctness-gone-mad Ron Atkinson. Whatever slings and arrows the metropolitan panjandrums of politeness may throw his way, Ron knows the after-dinner speaker invitation at our annual *Black & White Minstrel Burns Night Cabaret* is as solid as the marble-effect flooring in the Big Ron Wing of Ethnic Studies and Boutique Ownership in Sport.

Ron's contributions to the fields of men's outerwear and applied linguistics in football need no repetition, but it is less well known that he also pioneered the use of computers in coaching. As early as 1981, the then-Manchester United manager supervised the building of a sophisticated processing device to analyse tactical patterns. However, the machine was adjudged by the Old Trafford hierarchy to be dangerous, both due to the risk of electromagnetic waves destabilising Bryan Robson's delicate knees and because Bobby Charlton believed it to be the work of a witch.

Using connections to the Hong Kong underworld established during a pre-season tour of Asia with West Brom, Ron was able to house the apparatus in a Chinese restaurant in Altrincham. Working with Henry Lim, a waiter who had a degree in mathematics and a mah-jong habit, Ron inputted statistical information about every Division One player into a database. Processing power was provided by a ZX81 and the timer from a Goblin teasmaid, and the Ronotron 3000 outputted tactical advice in fortune cookie format.

Ron set great store by the predictions of the machine, accrediting it with masterminding his victory over Everton in the 1985 FA Cup Final. However, after celebrating that win with the squad, a hungry Ron arrived at the restaurant late at night and blundered into the kitchen in search of sweet and sour chicken. There he found Lim diligently writing nuggets of tactical advice on small slips of paper and inserting them into cookies. Ron had been taken for a ride. It was, he says, his lowest moment in football, and he turned his back on technology – and Chinese food – from that day forth, setting the application of computer modelling in football back by a generation.

TITO JACKSON MIDDLE SCHOOL
2000-2005 HAMILTON DRIVE, PLANO, TX

Report of _Lance Armstrong_   Class Teacher _James Dooley JKL_

Subject			Comments
SCIENCE	51	X	Lance always pays close attention in chemistry and makes sure to write down chemical formulas with great precision. His experimental work shows real potential.
	62		
	83		
VOLUN-TEERING			Lance always offers to take the school guinea pig home during vacations. The animal is "bulking up" at quite a speed, which Lance says is because he looks after it so good
ENGLISH	36		Lance's behaviour in the weekly 'show and tell' sessions has been unacceptable. any time a classmate attempts to speak, Lance leaps to his feet to shout "you're a liar", often with uncouth language.
	57		
	86		
MATH	1	1	Lance sadly seems to have problems remembering to turn up for tests making his boast "I have never failed" only part of the truth.
	0	1	
	1	1	
DRAMA			Our visiting drama teacher, Miss Winfrey, was moved to tears by the passion and sincerity of Lance's performance of the monologue: 'To be legally compelled to answer or not to be legally compelled to answer that is the question I shall be evading'.
FRENCH	5)	7)	Lance is very excited about the French exchange programme, but I am disturbed to hear him say he has heard "you can buy all sorts of cool stuff there and no one gives a rats ass
PHYSICAL EDUCATION	18	46	Lance shows admirable will to win but dressing up as a girl so as to "dominate and crush" on the kindergarten netball court is not playing nicely.
INTERACTION WITH OTHERS			Lance is a very generous young man, regularly offering out candy to others in the playground whether they want it or not.
HOMEROOM TEACHER'S COMMENTS			Lance usually has plenty to say for himself but I am concerned as to why he stubbornly refuses to answer any questions during our "What I Did On My Holidays" assignments.

Parent Signature ....   Date ....

75 School Report

Type and manuscript on paper
Texas, 1982

THE NEWS OF Lance Armstrong's fall from grace last year was met with dismay at the National Museum of the History of Sport, Orkney. The Museum's events coordinator and catering mastermind, Morag MacDonald, had been in correspondence with Armstrong's management about coming to do a summer workshop for young sporting historians on the island and, although there were some contractual issues to be ironed out (Armstrong's management wanted a cash payment of $100,000 for the afternoon; we offered a 15% discount in the Museum shop and as many visits to the refectory 'Sporty Soup Station' as Armstrong and his team wanted), we were confident that this great sporting hero would come and inspire the next generation.

There are many tragic aspects to Armstrong's disgrace, but perhaps none more bitter than the National Museum of the History of Sport, Orkney, having already printed out adverts about the cancelled event. Our cherished Sporty Soup Station, at least, remains inviolate from the cheat's hand, and perhaps many years from now, Armstrong will look back with regret at the missed chance to sample for himself Mrs MacDonald's famous Wildcat and Gorse Broth. It is his loss.

Not long after the calumny of Armstrong was finally laid bare in front of the world, the Museum received – anonymously – this 1982 school report about the young Texan. The only surprise is that it does not mention his wanton ingratitude towards his school's canteen staff.

PRODUCT OF AUSTRIA

Schloss
Schloshed

•

Gerecnraum
Geschlosschen

1985

ROTWEIN*

*Frostschutzmittel <5%

76 BBC Bottle

Glass, emptiness
White City, 1985

As a younger historian, I was briefly employed by the BBC. Thanks to my Scots heritage and an application form that may have given the impression I was disabled and a lesbian, I was fast-tracked by the Corporation as part of a diversity outreach programme. My first and – as it transpired – only posting was on the popular *A Question of Sport* quiz show, where I worked as a researcher with special responsibility for the Guess the Sportsman round.

However, the prestigious post was to have been merely a stepping stone for my ambition. I pitched to my superiors a concept for what would have been a magnificent series, sports history's *Civilisation* or *The World at War*. It was to be a documentary, narrated by myself, about the sex lives of famous sportsmen through the ages, with Linda Lusardi playing the roles of various sporting muses, lovers and conquests. Levity was to be added by comic segments involving Gary Wilmot as an incompetent butler. After initial support at the top level – Alan Yentob himself described the series as 'a truly astonishing idea' – the unaccountable corporate drones at the corporation clearly lost their bottle. It was quite clear to me that they simply did not have the boldness of vision needed to make my series; although I did also hear that Wilmot wanted too much money to come over from ITV.

I became disillusioned and vowed never again to waste an idea of that power and depth on the cowardly grey men of White City. This bottle pictured across the page was my only memento from my time there; I removed it from the *A Question of Sport* green room on my last day as a BBC employee. I confess I had been drinking and was emotional; in hindsight I can see why security thought I might by attempting to threaten Princess Anne with it. I was merely defending her honour against the cruel jibes of the late Emlyn Hughes.

Not a Wednesday evening goes past now without my watching *A Question of Sport* with hot tears of rage on my cheeks, an aching sorrow deep in my bowels and violent flashing images in my head, although I imagine I am not alone in that.

77 Miracle Toast

Partially burnt bread, divine intervention
Argentina, 1986

THE GLORIOUS PERFORMANCE by Diego Maradona in the 1986 World Cup generated a wave of near-hysterical joy in Argentina. It is no exaggeration to say that Maradona was regarded as something like a deity in the months that followed his effectively singlehanded triumph, and it was not long before odd Maradona-related phenomena began to be observed.

A girl in the northern Salta province said that Diego had appeared to her in a vision with a plan to win back Las Malvinas. An elderly man in Río Negro claimed to have been visited by an angel who told him that Diego was the Second Coming of Christ, but with a better left foot. And in Mendoza, a housewife removed this piece of bread from her toaster and was astonished to discover the face of Diego on the burned surface.

The Church in Argentina acted quickly to claim the Maradona Toast as a message from God. When further inspection revealed a stigmata-style blood-red teardrop on the bread, the Archbishop of Mendoza declared it to be a bona fide Miracle. Embarrassingly, after word had arrived back from Pope John Paul II approving the toast's status as a Living Holy Relic, it was discovered the stigmata was in fact a glob of strawberry jam. A feast day with a procession through the streets of Mendoza was downgraded to a really long church service in praise of the toast.

Right: Scientific analysis of the 'holy wholemeal' by the St. Augustine's Institute for Prandial Thaumaturgy (Brunch Branch) has revealed a flour mix rich in unusual grains, some from as far afield as Colombia. Maradona is himself said to have shown a keen interest in home baking; his Napoli team-mates have commented how they would often see him buying small bags of flour from local suppliers through the dressing-room window.

78 Swedish Furniture Designs

Wood-type substance, dowels, towels
Ljungby, 1987

IN THE 1980S, the Swedish FA was becoming concerned about the quality of players being produced by the country. The government agreed to partial funding of a national football academy, but insisted that the institution should generate its own revenue. Impressed by Roy Hodgson's work at Malmö, where he had significantly improved the design and aesthetics of the dressing-room and installed a walk-in wardrobe, Swedish FA chief Björn-Stakka Bø hit upon the idea of financing football development by the sale of affordable, self-assembly furniture.

Almost like a latter-day Bauhaus, young Swedish footballers were put to work designing and manufacturing the products in the morning, followed by football training, academic lessons and growing beards in the afternoon. Products such as the FLAT-PACK FOUR, the TORD right-hand cabinet and the ULRIKA fruit bowl sold in huge quantities, allowing the Academy to pour money back into research and development, culminating in the product line that would conquer the world: a huge, shiny self-reflecting mirror that recessed into its own bottom, the ZLATAN.

SVENNIS

ICKI ®

Lürv och Sexleksaker
ICKI av Sverige

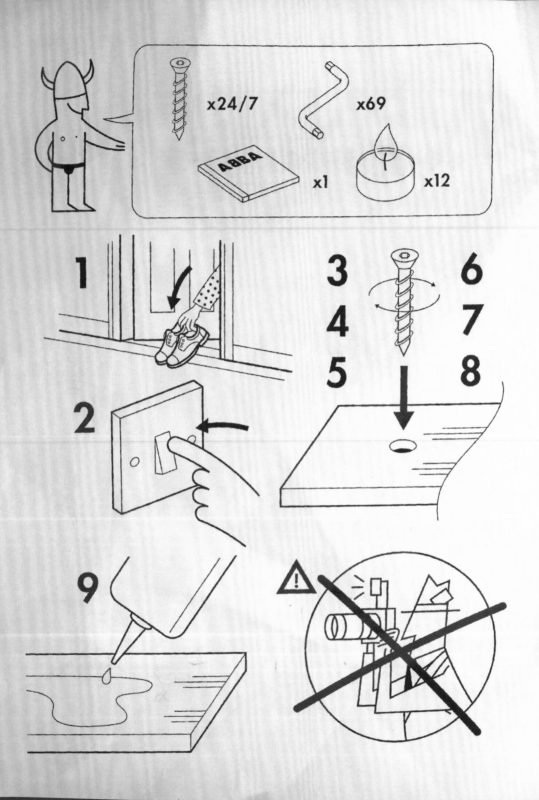

79 Demo Tape
Bury, 1989

A BOY'S BEDROOM. Bury. 1989. A 13-year-old bounces up and down on his Steve Bruce duvet cover, wrestling a screeching guitar solo out of his beloved Gibson Les Sealey guitar. His hair is parted in the sensible manner of his hero Mike Duxbury, but he wears the tight black jeans and ripped scarlet blouse of a 1970s rock god.

'Philip,' he yells. 'Philip, come in here and play on bass guitar.'
    A younger boy enters, dragging a too-large bass behind him.
    'I don't want to play rock and roll bands again, our Gary,' he says. 'I want to play working on my positioning at corners.'
    'Don't be soft, our Philip,' replies his brother. 'You've got a lot more chance of making it as a rock legend than you do as a footballer. Now go and get our Tracey and tell her to come and play drums on these Viv Anderson lunchboxes.'

The result of this bedroom 'jam session' is the demo tape above. Fusing his love of the Rolling Stones with his admiration for the uncompromising defending of Mal Donaghy, and drawing lyrical inspiration from the bullying he suffered at school for his nascent wispy moustache, Gary Neville created a collection of songs about restless youth, excess and how many sugars Alex Ferguson might take in his tea. He received no reply from any of the record companies to whom he sent the tape, save a threat of legal action from EMI if he contacted them again. Reluctantly, Gary decided to focus 110% on his football. Rock and roll's loss would be football's gain.

80 Soccer Skills Feature

Page from football magazine
Ventnor News & Tobacco, Isle of Wight, 1990

THIS 1990 boys' football magazine featured coaching advice from respected ex-players of the day. It is notable for containing the last explicitly football-related writing done by Davie Icke before his preoccupations turned away from sport.

The former Coventry City and Hereford United glovesman had been engaged by the publishers, Bush And Rothschild Press, to contribute to a book on soccer coaching. He was to have particular responsibility for the sections on goalkeeping, assisting on pictorial instructional spreads such as this one and writing an essay on the correct leisure attire for keeping goal.

Sadly, Icke became involved in a dispute with the publishers about image rights, copyright and the new world order, leading to his sections of the coaching manual being quietly dropped.

BACK TO SCHOOL!

#29 Defending Corners

1

Midfield players
defend penalty area zones

2

Wingback defends
near post

3

Centrebacks man-mark
tallest attackers

4

Manlizard eats
referee

Reader **COMPETITION!** Win a David Icke tracksuit! p88

81 Chess Notes

Nuggets of tactical genius on paper
Rotterdam, 1993

YOUTH, BRILLIANCE and a relentless hunger. Experience, a shellsuit, and the unwavering backing of Phil Neal. Kasparov versus Taylor in 1993 was a clash of personalities, of cultures, of beliefs, of systems. Of tactical superpowers.

Many expected that Taylor's depth of strategic sophistication would simply overwhelm the young Soviet. Taylor, needing just a draw as white in the critical Rotterdam game, began with a typically acute and elegant opening: the Carlton Palmer Gambit. Kasparov was visibly shaken by the sheer complexity of the Taylor thought processes.

When Taylor unleashed another magisterial manoeuvre, the 'Long bishop over the top', it seemed certain that the young pretender from Azerbaijan would be defeated, even humiliated. Then something quite remarkable happened. Taylor, looking to overwhelm Kasparov with his 'Get the queen up front and tell her to make a nuisance of herself' attack, blundered. Kasparov's pawn toppled Taylor's queen when it was nearly through the defence, but the match referee declined to intervene despite furious protests from Taylor. An irate Taylor threw his pieces on the floor and resigned.

Kasparov said: 'Obviously for me to lock horns with a tactical genius like Graham Taylor and come out on top is a fantastic result for me and obviously I'm over the moon.' The greatest strategist in history had been vanquished and was pilloried in the British press by having his head superimposed on a chess piece under the headline 'Red Hot Ruskie Pawn Star Beats Off Tayl'. Kasparov went on to immortality, and later the Bolton Wanderers hotseat.

G. Taylor	Kazza
Holland	

e4 d6

CAN WE NOT KNOCK IT?

Qh5 Nf6

DO I NOT LIKE THAT!

Qa5 Nc6

HIT LES! HIT LES!

Qg5 h6

THEY'VE DONE
EVERYTHING
THAT WE TOLD THEM
NOT TO DO.

Qe5 dxE5

WHAT SORT OF THING
IS HAPPENING HERE?

White resigns

TELL YOUR PAL THAT
HE'S JUST COST ME MY JOB

82 Barmy Army Knife

Metal penknife
Adelaide, 1995

DEVELOPED BY THE Barmy Army on the 1994–95 Ashes tour of Australia, this neat pocket knife contained all the equipment a cricket fan needed for a day's supporting England in hot and often hostile conditions.

The multi-tool came with a bottle opener, two spare bottle openers and a reserve spare bottle opener for use in emergencies. Knowing that thirst was the greatest enemy during a long overseas campaign, Barmy Army commanders also insisted on twin corkscrews. Other features included a tuning fork (tuned to a slightly off-key B-flat major) for starting a sing-song, a trumpet cleaning kit, a miniature flag of St George and a handy device for scratching hard-to-reach sunburnt areas.

The deluxe version included a blindfold to cover the eyes if an England batting collapse became too distressing, while later models included a laser for pointing out the unfortunate Mitchell Johnson.

A limited edition 'England Home' model, specially designed for use at Lord's, featured a retractable tie and contained a thousand pounds in tightly shrink-wrapped ten-pound notes, in case the owner wished to buy lunch from the food court.

THE LAWN TENNIS
CHAMPIONSHIP MEETING 1996

CENTRE COURT
ROYAL BOX
WEDNESDAY 3rd JULY

AVAILABLE ONLY FOR DAY
PRINTED HEREON

This badge does not admit to Ground

The entrance to the Royal Box
is on ground level

IMPORTANT — SEE OVER
NOT TRANSFERABLE

Tennis Championships
AS AND DESIGNATED AREAS

Richard

ONLY Gates
16, 17 or 19

s are bound by the
tions of Entry

EMERGENCY

In the event of illness or a
sudden urge to sing
CONTACT A MEMBER OF STAFF
or STEWARD / GUARD IMMEDIATELY

EVACUATION

In the event of prolonged
musical abuse it may be necessary
to evacuate you from your seat
Please take your microphone with you

SUPER
XXV
BOW

MARIA WHITMAN
WARDROBE ASS

PASS PASS PASS PASS

83 Press Passes

Printed accreditations, plastic sleeves, lanyards
South London, 1996

IN A LONG CAREER as an accredited member of the sporting media, I have been fortunate to witness some of the great contests of our age, many of them involving races to get to the subsidised press bar. I have collected my press passes from each and every event I have attended, with the exception of a World Cup 1994 identity card that snapped as Jack Charlton and I were trying to break into his hotel room with it.

I have also been fortunate to amass a collection of passes from major sporting figures and enthusiasts as diverse as Sir Mick Jagger, Alastair Campbell, Richard Hammond and Goonersaurus. Among my most treasured is this accreditation for the legendary 1996 impromptu Cliff Richard sing-song during a Wimbledon rain delay. I was unfortunately barred from the All England Club for the next decade, labouring as I was under the misapprehension that Sir Cliff was in fact Sir Tom Jones, and I deeply regret that I threw my underwear at him.

If only I had been in possession of a similarly easily-removable undergarment at the 2004 Super Bowl then perhaps poor Janet Jackson (a wonderful singer and a close personal friend) might not have been broken upon the wheel of public indignation merely for exposing herself to the world. I for one have lobbied repeatedly for more ladies to remove their intimates at the world's major sporting events, but sadly so far only the MCC have shown even the most guarded support.

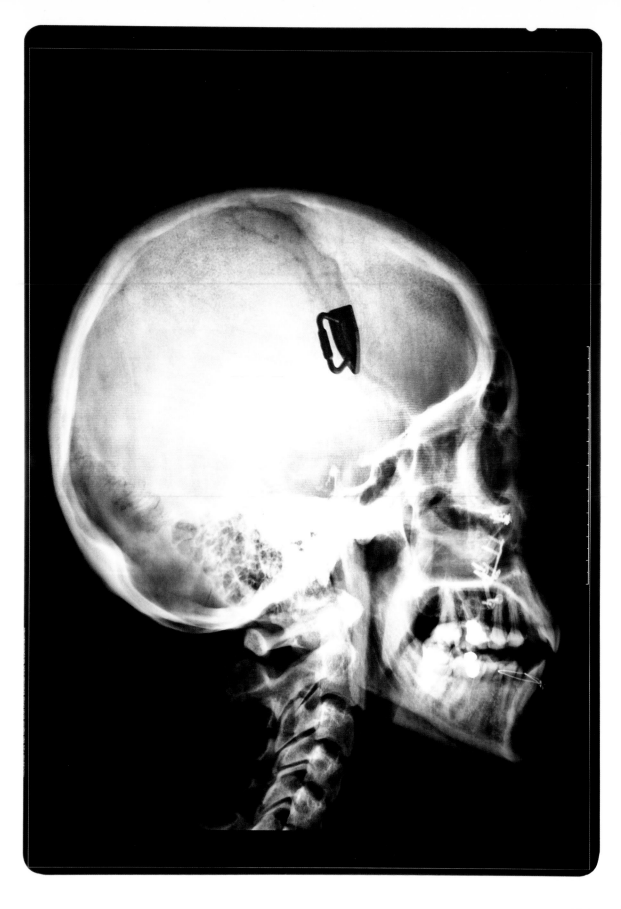

84 Iron Mike's Iron

Eponymous x-ray
Las Vegas, 1997

MIKE TYSON WAS arrested numerous times as a youngster and became so well known to police officers in his native Brooklyn precinct that they took to playing board games with him to pass the time while waiting for his public defender and youth offender caseworker. The young Tyson was extremely keen on Monopoly, but – displaying all the ferocious competitive instincts that would one day make him one of the most feared heavyweights of all time – he could not bear to lose.

While awaiting processing for a loitering charge in 1979, he appeared certain to be defeated in a game against Officer Rodriguez (playing as top hat), and possibly even trail into third place behind Officer Mahoney (little dog). Determined not to be bested, Tyson seized what pieces he could grab and began shoving them up his nose, hoping to have the game declared a no contest. Fortunately, he managed only the iron before the officers subdued him, but medical examination revealed that it would be impossible to remove the metal marker without potentially life-threatening surgery.

Throughout his teens and into adulthood, Tyson was troubled by the metal foreign body in his head. The iron picked up signals from local radio stations and also transmitted police frequencies, which gave him his nickname, and may in turn have contributed to his law-breaking ways. It is probable that he took to caring for pigeons because their soothing cooing noises drowned out the radio chatter and static. Research now suggests that the 1997 aberration in Las Vegas, in which Tyson bit Evander Holyfield in the notorious fight at the MGM Grand, may have been caused by sudden disorientation from a giant magnetic pulse emitted from the nearby Mirage, where Siegfried and Roy were performing an elaborate disappearing trick involving their white tiger, Derek, and a giant replica microwave oven.

85 Whingerbread Man

Baked voodoo gingerbread cookie dough, a pinch of salt
Brookline, Massachusetts, 1999

THE NOTORIOUS 1999 Ryder Cup in Massachusetts, which saw Colin Montgomerie relentlessly barracked by an unruly home support, provided excellent commercial opportunities for the local catering industry, with bakers doing especially well out of the tournament.

A craze sprang up for these Montgomerie 'Whingerbread Man' cookies, which were 'cursed' en masse in a colourful ceremony by an elderly Boston gypsy, to the delight of the partisan crowd. Over 10,000 were sold to American golf fans whose desire to see the unpopular Scot come a cropper on the course was matched only by their appetite for sugary snacks.

In a controversial publicity stunt, purchasers were encouraged to bite off the figurine's arms while the irascible Scots golfer was lining up a shot. Montgomerie was frequently distracted in mid-swing, although it is debatable whether this was due to the gypsy curse or the loud cracking sound made by the crunchy biscuits.

While his magnificent Ryder Cup record needs no sugar-coating, Montgomerie has admitted that he often becomes irritable around baked goods to this day, and once stormed out of a BBC interview when he was distracted by Steve Rider eating a Garibaldi biscuit in his eye line.

86 Blue Plaque

Ceramic disc with lettering, coats, pheremones
Knightsbridge, 1999

BORIS BECKER has accomplished many remarkable feats, including winning Wimbledon at the age of 17, retaining the title the next year under huge pressure of expectation, and successfully pretending to respect the opinion of British former tennis players as part of his role with the BBC. But surely none of his illustrious achievements can match that of taking less than five seconds to impregnate a stranger in a restaurant coat closet.

This plaque proudly hangs on the wall of the Nobu restaurant in London at the exact spot where the preternaturally potent German performed his celebrated cloakroom quickie. On a night out to celebrate his retirement from tennis, the German ace swept through the restaurant's stylish bar like a sexually engorged ginger Panzer division, latching efficiently onto a comely Russian model. Sadly, history does not relate the exact honeyed words that Herr Becker deployed upon the smitten young lady, only that he needed just a few moments to persuade her into congress in a convenient cupboard. Displaying the sort of explosive power which once earned him the nickname of 'Boom Boom', Boris was in and out as quickly as a British tennis player in the first round at Wimbledon, the consummation lasting an even shorter time than the courtship.

The restaurant briefly toyed with the idea of marketing a 'Becker Express' lunch menu for busy business clientele. However, with Nobu becoming a popular haunt for Premier League footballers, the eaterie opted instead for this plaque commemorating the Becker indiscretion and its subsequent expensive paternity ramifications *pour encourager les autres*.

87 Rosette

Pleated ribbon, hot foil blocking, injured pride
Didsbury, 2002

ONE OF MANCHESTER UNITED's Official Charity Partners (Local) for the 2002 season was Didsbury's Alright, Pet – a petting zoo where shy local children could play with farm animals and build confidence from the bonds they formed, as well as meeting some of their football heroes. After an embarrassing pre-season incident where Roy Keane had berated a sheep for its 'sloppy, lazy attitude', the club discreetly ensured that only suitable players attended the monthly sessions at the farm.

Paul Scholes proved to be the best in the role, apart from one wild tackle on a goose, and became the club's 'Zoo Captain'. Under his quiet but determined leadership, dozens of local kids enjoyed stroking the animals for an hour or so twice a month, before a kickabout and some prawn sandwiches.

Sadly, the partnership was short-lived. The zoo's Vice President (Ruminant Division) was a diehard United fan; he asked if Ruud Van Nistelrooy, his favourite player, might come down for a day. The free-scoring Dutchman agreed, and enjoyed a warm September afternoon at the zoo with children from nearby Saint Bryan's Primary. However, the zoo's main field had, due to a mix-up, been double-booked with a local pony club show. As he was leaving the zoo to get into his Bentley Arnage, an excited horse-mad young girl ran up to Van Nistelrooy and stuck a rosette on him. The PFA Player of the Year was furious to win Runner-Up in the 'Best Groomed Horse' category and, even though the girl, the pony club and the zoo rightly claimed that it had been an honest mistake, the humiliated Van Nistelrooy vowed to demand a transfer if the club continued its relationship with the zoo.

Alex Ferguson could not risk alienating his best goalscorer and had no choice but to acquiesce. Van Nistelrooy later wrote in his autobiography *Dutch Picnic*: 'I was ashamed and outraged, very upset. I definitely should have won first place.'

88 Fertility Idol

Priapic tribal fetish
Brazil, 2003

DEEP IN THE RAINFOREST of Brazil, the Weinerinho tribe had remained uncontacted for generations until a small light aircraft crashed near their settlement. While this was tragic for those onboard (there were no survivors), it was a wonderful moment for sports historians and leisure anthropologists.

One of the unfortunate passengers had with him a laptop and, from what we can gather, a tribesman managed to turn it on. It appears that the first contact the Weinerinho had with the outside world was of a pop-up advert featuring Pelé advertising Viagra.

The Weinerinho – a mobile, aggressive hunter-gatherer people – had seen their numbers dwindle to a few dozen due to the effects of chronic impotence, probably caused by a diet lacking in haggis. Luckily, within a few weeks they were receiving thousands of emails a week offering a cure for erectile dysfunction and a safe online ordering procedure that enabled them to have the life-changing product delivered within a matter of days.

Their chief commissioned a statue of Pelé, who came to be revered as the deity Vi'Ag'Ra, in celebration of the newly-acquired wonder drug. Their vigour renewed thanks to the football legend and his little blue pills, several of the Weinerinho set off for nearby towns and cities, trading statues of the football legend in exchange for cooling ointments. It was in nearby Joaõn River that the Museum acquired this example.

Right: An exact-scale replica of the Vi'Ag'Ra totem. I am grateful to the children of Egilsay Infant School for their help in reconstructing this exhibit. The original, made from carved mahogany and piranha bone, was accidentally dropped in the Westray Firth while on its way to a 'Maps & Baps' barbecue organised as part of our community outreach programme.

89 Advertising Slogan

Magic marker on Post-It
Soho, 2004

AT THE National Museum of the History of Sport, Orkney, we welcome many young schoolchildren a year and, as such, are no strangers to the occasional 'accident'. For this reason, there was nothing but sympathy in our marbled (and recently disinfected) corridors when Wee Paula Radcliffe was unfortunately 'taken short' during the 2004 women's Olympic Marathon.

Paula has long been a friend to the Museum – she regards our toilet facilities as among the best and most clearly signposted of any public building in the Islands – and she was kind enough personally to donate this next object.

After her roadside comfort break in Athens, several advertising agencies pitched campaigns, hoping to ride on the coat-tails of Paula's movement. The one that came closest to seeing the light of day was this, in which Paula's admirably slim figure and legendarily quick metabolism were to form the basis of a promotion for a controversial diet supplement: Nutri-Evac.

Unhappily, the European Courts found that the product's efficacy in promoting weight loss was a result of it being entirely composed of horse laxative, and that even a modest dosage caused the user to void out not just the contents of the stomach but sometimes the stomach itself. Fortunately, the product was quietly shelved before serious damage was done to either public health or Paula's good name.

Right: The advertising agency Halford, Downing, Tipton & Hill achieved further notoriety two years later when, now known as HDTH-ADHD, they masterminded a strategy placing Steve McClaren as the new face of Chanel. The campaign failed dismally and all the partners retired to Provence on the proceeds.

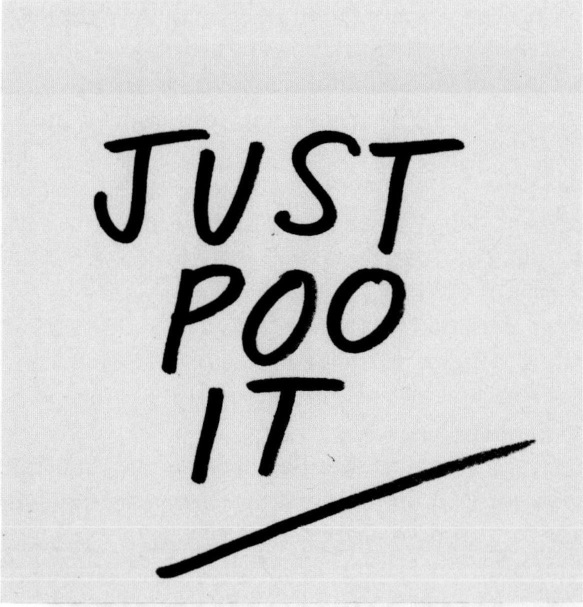
JUST
POO
IT

90 Musical Theatre Poster

Lithographic inks on paper
North Norfolk, 2006

THE CONSOLING HANDSHAKE given by Andrew Flintoff to Brett Lee in the 2005 Ashes Test at Edgbaston was not just a shining example of sportsmanship but the catalyst for what might have been one of musical theatre's greatest triumphs. Sadly, it proved to be the genesis of one of its most notorious commercial disasters.

Inspired by the Lee–Flintoff moment of bonding, Norfolk composer and keen cricket fan Keith Lloyd Webber (no relation to the more famous Andrew) wrote a musical in which Lee and Flintoff were imagined as two star-crossed lovers on opposite sides of a bitter feud. Lloyd Webber (no relation) fought a protracted legal battle with the copyright holders of the *West Side Story* musical and eventually had to concede that his production would only be allowed to go ahead if the two male leads had their voices drowned out by white noise at every performance. This was considered somewhat draconian, but a legal ruling that the actors playing the parts of Flintoff and Lee had to wear gags so that audiences could not even watch them mime surely bordered on the vindictive.

The show opened in Hunstanton's famous North End in November 2006, to mixed reviews. The *Daily Mail's* Baz Bamigboye, disorientated by the cacophony of high-decibel industrial noises that dominated act one and, apparently confused as to which musical he was watching, wrote in his review 'It's Buddy painful'. Sadly, this was the most charitable assessment from a member of the press and as such had to form a major part of the publicity campaign.

All this notwithstanding, however, there was still some muted public interest, but this soon evaporated once Steve Harmison got to work in Brisbane. The show closed after just one day of the first Test, and Lloyd Webber (no relation) took a break from show business altogether. He is rumoured to be working on a musical about the golden age of Australian swing called *Five Guys Named Merv* and is currently seeking investors and legal representation.

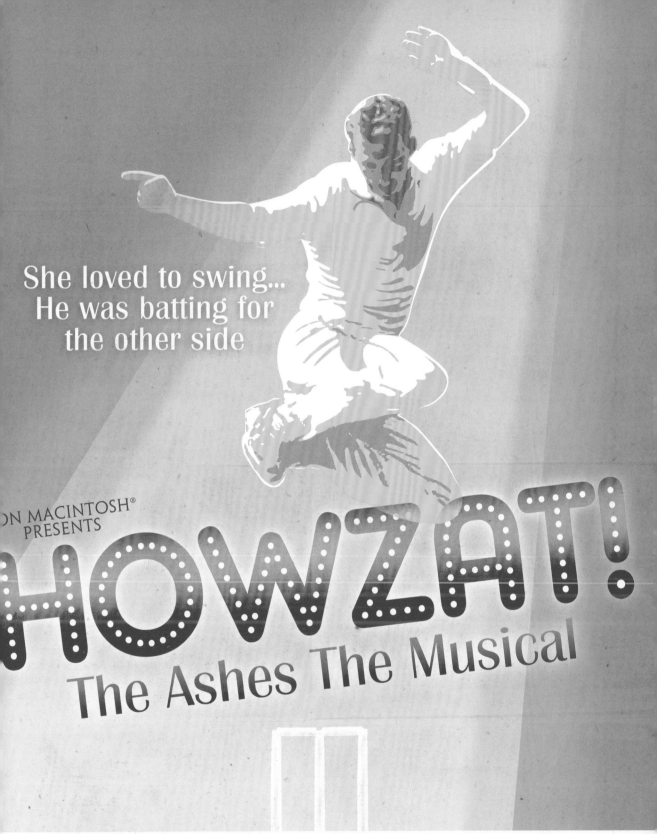

She loved to swing...
He was batting for
the other side

ON MACINTOSH® PRESENTS

HOWZAT!

The Ashes The Musical

SEATS AVAILABLE FOR ALL PERFORMANCES

Theatre Royal Hunstanton

BOX OFFICE HOTLINE 01486 533576 (10AM-4PM) TICKETS £8 CONC £6

91 Banksy Self-portrait

Hand-cut stencil and spray paint on brick
Leicester, 2007

THE 2007 APPEARANCE of this mural definitively settled one of the most speculated-upon questions in modern art: the identity of Banksy.

Painted on the wall of a gentleman's outfitters in Leicester, this vibrant, challenging work depicts the artist performing his most storied save, the incredible one-handed flick to deny Pele's header at the 1970 World Cup in Mexico. The pineapple is thought to be a satirical representation of the Iraq War, or perhaps a comment on Peter Shilton.

Having jealously guarded his anonymity for so long, it was a surprise to many when Banksy chose to apparently 'out' himself as the former England goalkeeper. However, when viewed in the light of this picture, the contention that they are one and the same is unanswerable.

The mural appeared in August 2007, 40 years to the day after the great goalkeeper was sold by Leicester City to Stoke City. A local newspaper interview with Banks revealed that he had returned to the East Midlands city in 2007 to give an after-dinner speech to the Worshipful Company of Pet Shop Owners (Leicester), putting him in the area at the time the mural appeared. As a much-loved local celebrity, he would have had easy access to aerosol paints at either B&Q or Wickes branches nearby, possibly even at a discount. Perhaps most telling of all, the World Cup winner was often pictured wearing gloves, probably to keep tell-tale paint off his hands.

The artist known as Banksy has concerned himself with themes of urban alienation, unfeeling capitalism, surveillance society and changes to the back-pass rule. It now appears that he was active for a far longer period than first supposed, probably from around the time of England's return from Mexico 1970. That Banksy chose not to produce any of his distinctive artwork until the turn of the millennium is testament to the professionalism and amount of preparation that goes into making his trademark stencils.

92 Tea Towel

Water-based inks on Belfast linen
St John's Wood, 2009

THE MUSEUM IS GRATEFUL to our generous corporate partners
Barstarde Capital for their continuing investment in this section
of the exhibition. They have been tremendous supporters of the
National Museum of the History of Sport, Orkney, and we were
delighted to host the recent conference launch of their consumer
banking division's new slogan ('We listen to you: you work for us
for the rest of your life').

In association with other corporate supporters (including
management consultants Logofiddle-Sackem and the insurance
giant Ipswich Weasel), the Museum produced this specially
commissioned range of tea-towels ideal for mopping up spilled
Bollinger on a corporate day out.

CRICKET HOSPITALITY

as explained to a corporate visitor.

Play is either on or off. If more off than on
drink on, but drink off and on when on-off and only
drink on and on if play is off off.

The lights may be on or off, or off then on.
Regardless, all play on until play is off, all
then go off but you may carry on.

If in doubt, drink on.

Staff are on-hand, unless they are off, although you
may find them off-hand if on when play is off.

Finally, we regret to inform you that while the chicken
is on, the salmon is off.

That's the end of the jolly

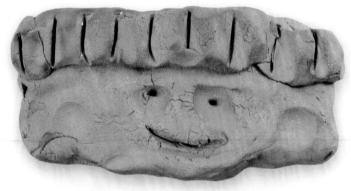

93–95 Big Man Moka

Tribal haircare gifts
Mount Hagen, Papua New Guinea, 2011

THESE CHARMING CLAY 'portraits' were made by tribal artists after a Manchester United pre-season tour to Papua New Guinea. Always eager to expand into new markets, the club played some friendly matches, and enjoyed brisk sales of replica shirts. The island custom of 'Big Man Giving' or 'Moka' – where prestige is demonstrated by making increasingly lavish gifts to one's associates – saw high-status Papua New Guineans (or 'Big Men') competing to get the longest possible name printed on the back of a jersey. Giving a replica strip with 'Nani' or 'Bebe' on it was considered a grave slight.

Interestingly, many of the Manchester United players carried the Moka custom back to England, and for some weeks afterwards scarcely a day would go past at the Carrington training ground without a Rio Ferdinand or a Ryan Giggs giving a junior team-mate a Rolls Royce or a Cheshire mansion in order to assert dominance.

Wayne Rooney was a big hit in Papua New Guinea and locals were fascinated by his regenerating hairline. He was given the Tok Pisin language nickname 'Big fella spudface har come bak' – 'Big Man with a manly jawline whose hair seems to be growing back'. These portraits (*left*) captured the English forward at three stages of the hair-restoring process, and for a while there was a fashion for thinning the hair to look like Rooney. Had it not been for a misunderstanding with an elderly tribeswoman and a large amount of cash, his popularity there would surely be undimmed today.

96 Equine DNA

Scientific data schematic
Blackpool University of Animal Science (Tesco Campus), 2012

IT WAS LONG TAKEN as certain fact that all Thoroughbred racehorses were descended from just three stallions, those imported into England from the Middle East in the early 18th century. However, new findings by a remarkable – some say 'renegade' – equine geneticist explode this myth.

Shunned by the horseracing establishment, the scientific community and even his own family, Dr Les Latchford, MSc (Oxon) (Croydon Campus) (Online)* has made it his life's work to prove the existence of an additional stallion. In his 1,024-page self-published paper on the subject: *Forgotten Horse – A Fourth Shooter?* Dr Latchford proves, via DNA sampling, archive research and studying the form in the *Racing Post*, that there is another, entirely separate bloodline.

According to Latchford, the original three horses (the Byerley Turk, the Darley Arabian and the Godolphin Arabian) were joined by a fourth imported Arabian stallion: the Omar Sharif. Latchford concedes that the offspring of Omar Sharif may not be quite of the same calibre as the other three – a descendant is yet to win a horserace – but he is convinced that some of the nicest donkeys on Blackpool beach are of the bloodline, and is lining up a big Grand National day accumulator involving Sharif progeny that he is convinced will prove him right once and for all, in addition to providing enough funds to carry out essential renovations on his caravan-laboratory.

* awaiting results of stewards' enquiry

```
BUAS _ TESCO _ RUN _ LOG
ADN-RUNWAY-22
TT-HOR53.SH.T

CONTRIBUTOR X
DB61 _ 59332-1
HAPLOGROUP : D0B81N

PHENOTYPIC _ UUC _ F _ OMAR _ SHARIF

OMAR SHARIF
==OMAR LITTLE
==I SHOT THE SHARIF
==ORIGINAL GANGSTER
==ORIGINAL NUTTER
==ORIGINAL RECIPE BRIGADIER GERRARD
==STEVEN GERRARD
==GERRARD'S CROSS
==GERRARD'S MISSED IT
==GERRARD'S BLOODY FURIOUS
==  ==ARKLE
==  ==SPARKLE
==  ==TARKLE
==  ==TARKA THE OTTER
==  ==HARRY POTTER
==  ==HARI KRISHNA
==  ==KRISHNAN GURU-MURTHY
==  ==  ==  --DESERT ORCHID
==  ==  ==  ==DESSERT ORCHID
==  ==  ==  ==TESCO VALUE DESSERT ORCHID
==  ==  ==  ==BLACK BEAUTY
==  ==  ==  ==BLACK BETTY
==  ==  ==  ==SWEATY BETTY
==  ==  ==  ==  ==  ==  ??  ==RED RUM
==  ==  ==  ==  ==  ==  ==RED ROSE
==  ==  ==  ==  ==  ==  ==ROSY POSY
==  ==  ==  ==  ==  ==  ==NOSEY PARKER
--  --  --  --  --  --  --SARAH JESSICA PARKER
==  ==  ==  ==  ==  ==  ==  ==SHERGAR
==  ==  ==  ==  ==  ==  ==  ==BURGAR (BY TESCO OUT OF BARBEQUE)
==  ==  ==  ==  ==  ==  ==  ==UNNAMED BLACKPOOL DONKEY
==  ==  ==  ==  ==  ==  ==  ==BONGO'S JETPACK
==  ==  ==  ==  ==  ==  ==  ==PRINCESS ANNE
==  ==  ==  ==  ==  ==  ==  ==JACKET BY ZARA (STRONGLY FANCIED)
```

97 Buddhist Swimming Frog

Wood, gold leaf, lead paints, lacquer
High Temple, Bal Timor, 2012

THIS STATUE is a treasure from an obscure sect of Buddhism that venerates the Buddha as a blissful, swimming frog. It was kindly loaned by the Phelps Museum, Maryland.

The monks at the Bal Timor temple believe that the tranquillity and freedom that come from swimming enable the spirit to find release and enlightenment. It is important to prepare for swimming by meditating in total silence, undisturbed, hence the 'headphones' worn by the Frog Buddha as it contemplates underwater nirvana.

Interestingly, the sect encourages a diet that is surprisingly high in junk food, importing processed cheese and crisps into its hilltop retreat. The swimming frog monks favour the use of medicinal herbs to promote serenity, and giggling; and also the channelling of calm through listening to the hypnotic, repetitive 'bong' of a deep, solitary bell.

98 Energy Drink

Carbonated water, sugar, caffeine, ginseng, herring
London via Stockholm, 2012

THIS IS A SAMPLE of the official energy drink of the Swedish 2012 Olympic women's handball team. While the team may not have performed well on the court (played five, lost five) they were singled out for praise by the Official Athletes' Committee for their 'boundless enthusiasm and friendliness' around the Olympic Village.

The team's coach had worked with a small soft-drink manufacturer in Ljungby to develop a limited-edition refreshment product that would, without recourse to any illegal or banned substances, offer his team a boost in refuelling and recovery.

'That didn't really work,' said Coach Magnus Gettinmysson, who kindly agreed to a short interview with the National Museum of the History of Sport, Orkney, as well as even more kindly sending some photographs of the women's handball team training. 'They didn't really get any better at handball.'

'But what a great bunch of girls,' he added. 'Great.'

We at the Museum tested the Bølt! soft drink and found it to contain a mixture of caffeine, pickled herring, spring water and an unidentified psychoactive ingredient that made our laboratory technician, Agnes, 'feel funny'.

I can confirm that her behaviour did indeed become excitable. On behalf of the Museum, I am now lobbying the Scottish Parliament to pump funding into handball refreshment research in the Orkneys without delay.

Röllmop
Smak!

BØLT!

Nu med Ginseng!

Lightning Energy Drink
Blixtnedslag Energidryck

För vältränade killar och tjejer | Kommer
hålla dig uppe hela natten | För fit boys
& girls | Keep it up all night

99 Home Entertainment System

Precious metals, nuclear material, cheese
Dallas, 2013

THIS EXTRAORDINARY ITEM is testament not just to sporting greatness, innovation and good taste, but also to friendship. The Dennis Rodman Home Entertainment Chandelier was personally designed by North Korean President Kim Jong-Un and presented to his close associate, the former NBA All-Star Dennis Rodman.

It comprises a giant crystal light fixture approximately 35 feet in diameter, constructed of gold, plutonium, diamonds and tiny statuettes of the Supreme Leader carved from what appears to be hard cheese, possibly pecorino. It features a basketball hoop in the centre which acts as a trigger; if a ball is shot through the basket the unit descends from the ceiling, fanning out eight 'limbs'. It was first thought that Kim Jong-Un had based the design on a spider but arachnids have been banned in North Korea during his entire adult lifetime, making it more likely that Kim Jong-Un was inspired by watching Rodman participate in a tag-team wrestling contest in which all four participants grappled on the floor at the same time.

The 'limbs' then hydraulically fan out and raise up to form an entirely enclosed pod in which Rodman can sit. Inside the pod is a comfortable reclining chair made from titanium and mink, a television, games console and soft-play area, signed pictures of Kim Jong-Un and Rodman playing basketball, tennis, Cluedo and dress-up, as well as a small refrigerator with some kimchi, thoughtfully provided for Rodman if he gets hungry. The unit is cleaned and maintained by two lightweight metal and sapphire robots modelled exactly on the naked forms of LA Laker Girls. Its value is estimated at $100 million and it was recently featured on an episode of the *MTV Cribs* spin-off show *MTV Light Fittings*.

**The Dennis Rodman Home
Entertainment Chandelier**

NMFTHOSO/P312.3

REMOVED FOR CLEANING

LTA : 1602.3

07-NOV-13

ROYAL WIMBLEDON HOSPITAL

14 : 28 : 01

DR WADE

41 / 42 PWR : 90

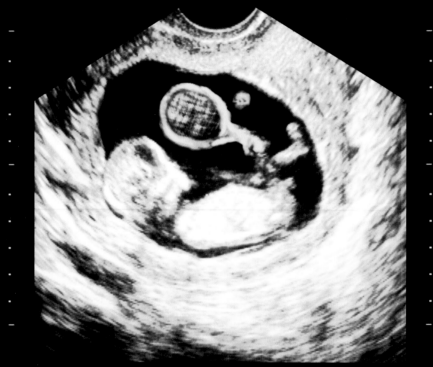

GA=12w3d   62mm/1.3   6-0 6-0 / SW19

100 The Sports Star of the Future

Ultrasound scan
Womb, 2013

IN THIS EXHIBITION, we have seen how treasures from antiquity to the present day have enriched sport and been integral to the stories of sportsmen and women. But what will life be like for the sports star of the future?

Cutting-edge research at the Orkney Institute of Human/Animal Sciences and Ceilidh Management suggests that the next big developments in sports conditioning and training will take place prior to birth.

Parents eager for their child to make progress on the tennis circuit are beginning to train the baby *in utero*. Here we see a promising young female player already practising her forehand passing shot and grunting. The Lawn Tennis Association has invested some £300 million in an ante-natal coaching unit to be headed up by Jeremy Bates, although sadly – as yet – British tennis foetuses are being outclassed by hungrier unborn children from less well-resourced countries.

The rewards for the sporting greats of tomorrow will be enormous. Sponsors are already keen to track the progress of potential charismatic future stars in a variety of sports, with Rory McIlroy's multi-million-dollar Nike deal believed to include a clause that any future child will exit the host mother's birth canal in a Nike cap. From the USA, we are seeing reports of college football teams attempting to recruit athletes with strong DNA athletic indicators prior even to the moment of conception, offering financial incentives to procreating parents in exchange for a verbal commitment on behalf of their foetus, most controversially in the case of the as-yet-to-be-conceived D'Brickashaw Gatorade Randell Ell, a future starting linebacker with the University of Michigan.

In Conclusion…

I AM STANDING at the top of the staircase at the National Museum of the History of Sport, Orkney, its elegant slow sweep leading down onto the expansive marble-floored lobby below. It is the opening-night reception of *Tutenkhamen's Tracksuit: The History of Sport in 100ish Objects*. I take a sip of our excellent locally produced Sauvignon Blanc 'Orkfire' – perhaps a little on the minerally side for some palates but I think both refreshing and bracing – and allow myself a small moment of proud satisfaction in this rare moment of solitude. The exhibition that has been my life's work, finally brought to fruition.

A look around the guests and dignitaries below reveals a who's-who of British sport. Kris Akabusi there, his distinctive roaring laugh echoing across the room as he shares an anecdote with John Terry. John now moving away across the lobby with a turn of pace that many felt had deserted him during his latter seasons at Chelsea. Over by the buffet table – where Mrs MacDonald has excelled herself with her razor-clam bake and venison profiteroles – none other than Geoffrey Boycott, filling up a Tupperware container that he had presumably brought in underneath his windcheater. Getting Geoffrey to come was something of a coup: once we had agreed to Sky+ *CSI: Miami* for him at 9pm and let him watch it in the security guard's office immediately after the reception, and paid for a helicopter back to his holiday home in the Ardèche, he accepted the invitation with pleasure. Ryan Giggs there, with a pretty lady I assume to be Mrs Giggs, or at least *a* Mrs Giggs, standing shyly off to one side, still coltish at 40 even though those temples are now greying somewhat. The march of time, the comet trail of history. I follow Ryan's gaze over to the main entrance, where the guest of honour is arriving. A discreet but unmistakeable frisson of excitement flutters through the room: Sir Alex Ferguson enters, cheerfully greeting members of the local press with a volley of abuse. He stops to sign an autograph or two and collars a drinks waiter. Sir Alex, an old friend, looks up to the balcony and catches my eye, raises his glass with a nod of approval. His blessing for our exhibition means a great deal.

But mighty though the master manager's achievements have been, they are but a ripple on the lake of sporting history, a few neat chisel marks on the glorious bust of sporting time. I close my eyes again and inhale deeply, thinking back through the thousands of objects my team considered for inclusion in the exhibition, the years of archiving, of unearthing, of discovering. The awe-inspiring responsibility of attempting to tell the story of sport's heroes and villains, its leaps of progress and its disasters, its power to unite and to enrage. To play the midwife for these stories of the innovators and pioneers whose deeds and words have shaped sport, and thus shaped human life – it has been both humbling and exhilarating.

I exhale, and open my eyes. Far over to the right I can see Colin Montgomerie, moodily sipping a cup of tea, alone, dunking a biscuit. He smiles politely but unwelcomingly as the large, gregarious figure of Big Sam Pilkington looms into view, and coolly declines his offer of a sausage roll. Pilkington, not the sensitive type, shrugs and shovels the pastry into his mouth, leaving a good portion of it on his cheeks and whiskers, before noting approvingly some members of the Swedish women's handball team who are giggling at something the Milanese monk Friar Silvio has whispered to them. Over by the bar, Dante is demonstrating his short-iron play to Henry VIII, who is suggesting a more closed stance and a chop down on the ball; their discussion is interrupted by William Webb Ellis, who has lined up shots of flaming Sambuca for the three of them and Heracles, who seems flushed and excitable and had just pushed in front of Paula Radcliffe in the queue for the lavatory. In the centre of the room, alone and smiling serenely, stands the slight figure of Tutenkhamen, resplendent in his burial tracksuit, a still, divine calm at the eye of this storm of timeless sporting greatness. He points at me, spreads his arms in an expansive gesture of congratulation and communion, and beckons.

I close my eyes.

Gideon Rupert

Acknowledgements

With thanks to Charlotte Atyeo.

Thanks to esteemed colleagues Professor Jon Horsley, chair of Applied Cricket at the Finchley Institute, and Dr John Nicholson, visiting fellow of Meat History at the University of Norfolk.

Van Nistelrooy rosette kindly loaned from the Hilary Butler collection. Whingerbread man kindly supplied by Asker's of Stamford.

The authors and publisher gratefully acknowledge permission to reproduce the material contained in this book and the relevant rights holders are acknowledged below. Every effort has been made to trace and contact copyright holders. If there are any inadvertent omissions we apologise to those concerned and will undertake to include suitable acknowledgements in all future editions.

Photography and artwork © Alan Tyers and Beach
Dinosaur illustration © Lucy Evans
Big Man Moka portraits © Katie Evans / Lucy Evans

The following pictures were adapted from images in the public domain or released under a Creative Commons license:

Big Bang original image by ESA/Hubble/NASA
FA Cup record from an original image by Mediatus
Roman bust by Sailko
Chegwin's owl by Green Lane
Nautical chart by Geographicus Rare Antique Maps
Lakeside Tapestry by Myrabella
C-90 cassette by Joxemai
Mayan Codex by the Walters Art Museum

The following images incorporate works licensed by istockphoto:

Amoeba photomicrograph / Cave interior / Head Down Man /
Tutenkhamen / Calyxurea / Gladiatorial Mosaic / Wrestler's Tale
Flying Franc / Beaver Totem / Holy Frijoles / Pop Art Prints
Iron Mike X-ray / Bolt Energy Drink

No children or animals were harmed in the making of this book,
although one or two gingerbread men have been eaten.

Further Reading

Tyers, Alan B., & Beach. *W.G. Grace Ate My Pedalo*. John Wisden & Co., Alton, Hampshire 2010

Tyers, Alan B., & Beach. *CrickiLeaks: The Secret Ashes Diaries*. John Wisden & Co., Alton, Hampshire 2011

Tyers, Alan B., & Beach. *Gin & Juice: The Victorian Guide to Parenting*. Bloomsbury, London 2012

Tyers, Alan B., & Beach. *I Kick Therefore I Am*. Bloomsbury, London 2012

Tyers, Alan B., & Beach. *Who Moved My Stilton?: The Victorian Gi*

796.0207 TYERS
Tyers,
Tutenkhamen's tracksuit :
R2000727459 WOLF CREEK

ODC

Atlanta-Fulton Public Library